FLIRTING
with
FRENCH

· ·

Adventures in Pursuit of a Language

· ·

by WILLIAM
ALEXANDER

Duckworth Overlook

First published in the US and UK 2015 by
Duckworth Overlook

LONDON
30 Calvin Street, London E1 6NW
T: 020 7490 7300
E: info@duckworth-publishers.co.uk
www.ducknet.co.uk
For bulk and special sales, please contact
sales@duckworth-publishers.co.uk
or write to us at the address above

NEW YORK
141 Wooster Street, New York, NY 10012
www.overlookpress.com

A catalogue record for this book is available
from the British Library

ISBN 978-0-7156-4995-4

Printed and bound in the UK

For Guy

God was easier to understand than French.

—Singer Pearl Bailey,
explaining why she dropped a French class to take up theology

CONTENTS

· · · · · · · · · · · · · · · ·

FLIRTING WITH FRENCH

La France, Mon Amour

. . . .

French, for me, is not just an accomplishment. It's a need.

—ALICE KAPLAN, *French Lessons*, 1994

Last night I dreamt I was French.

This mainly involved sipping absinthe at the window of a dark, chilly café, wrapped in a long scarf that reached the floor, legs crossed, Camus in one hand and a hand-rolled cigarette in the other. I don't remember speaking French in the dream, and just as well, for in real life I once grandly pronounced in a Parisian restaurant, "I'll have the ham in newspaper, and my son will have my daughter."

I love France. I have from the first time I stepped onto its soil as a twenty-two-year-old with nothing more than a backpack and a Eurail pass, and subsequent visits over thirty-five years have only fueled my passion. What's to love?

- A summer day along the Seine, the riverbank alive with groups of young people talking, singing, dancing, and sunning. Outrageously and playfully, the Seine has been transformed by Paris's popular socialist mayor into a city-long beach, complete with sprinklers and tons of sand.

- Sitting at the counter of an astoundingly good restaurant alongside an elderly Frenchman and his white miniature poodle, for whom he has ordered a *bifteck*, rare. The server, who speaks no English, is practically begging me to order an off-the-menu special, which, as far as I can make out with my mostly forgotten high school French, is either young milk-fed pig or young pig marinated in milk, or both. The server prevails, and it is, as he knew it would be, the best meal I have ever eaten.

- Traveling from the Mediterranean to Paris by train at 190 miles an hour, the window turned into a fast-motion scroll of medieval villages, farms, and pastures.

- The owner-chef of a small village inn who, having just prepared and served us pigeon, rabbit, and foie gras, comes outside to help us clear an unexpected frost from our rental car windshield with the only tool available, her credit card.

- The hush of dawn at a medieval monastery, for a magical ten minutes perhaps the most beautiful spot anywhere on earth, as the Norman mist vaporizes before my eyes, lifting its veil from rows of sunlit apple and pear trees, their ripe fruit awaiting the attention of a monk's hands and a chef's knife.

· A hole-in-the-wall Latin Quarter brasserie you won't find in any guidebook, whose waiter, a dead ringer for Teller (of Penn and Teller), skids around the sawdust-covered floor like Charlie Chaplin, balancing platters of *saumon à la crème* with crispy *pommes frites* (fifteen dollars, dessert included).

· A rainy afternoon with my wife at a Left Bank brasserie, watching the city scurry home, the drizzly streets an impressionist canvas come to life, Anne and I drunk on cold beer, on Paris, on love, happy as happy gets, neither of us speaking much, just enjoying the scene and realizing how lucky we are to love the same things, and Paris, and each other.

France does that to you.

Some Americans want to visit France. Some want to live in France. I want to *be* French. I have such an inexplicable affinity for all things French that I wonder if I was French in a former life (I'd like to think Molière, but with my luck, more likely Robespierre, which explains that persistent crick in my neck). I love French music and movies. I yearn to play *boules* in a Provençal village square while discussing French politics. To retire to a little pied-à-terre in the city or a stone *mas* in the country. To get to know and understand the people who still worship Napoleon, who consider "philosopher" a job title, who can be both maddeningly rigid and movingly gracious, and who can send their children away at age fourteen to be apprentices.

Most of all, I yearn to bring sound—speech—to that quiet café of my dream. I can't be French if I don't speak French. It's time to stop yearning and start learning. True, at fifty-seven I'm well into what is politely referred to as late middle age, and my goal of fluency in French won't come easily. But the way I look at it, next year I'll be fifty-eight, and it won't be any easier then. *C'est la vie.*

Stiff Job

· ·

Pickering: we have taken on a stiff job.
—HENRY HIGGINS, on Eliza Doolittle, *Pygmalion*, 1912

There aren't too many places where you can hear a joke like this while standing in line for coffee: "So, I'm lecturing my class last week. In the English language, I tell them, a double negative forms a positive. However, in some languages, such as Russian, a double negative remains a negative. But there isn't a single language, not one, in which a double positive can express a negative. And I hear a voice from the back of the room: 'Yeah, right.'"

Certainly I'm not at Starbucks. This is the thirty-third annual Second Language Research Forum, or SLRF, which everyone here just calls "slurf," at the University of Maryland. I've come in the hope of getting some insight and advice for the task that I am about to tackle: learning French—becoming *fluent* in French—at the age of fifty-seven. The opening speaker, Michael Long, a professor of second-language acquisition at the University of Maryland and the author of several books on the subject, has just told the 250 assembled linguists (although he seems to be looking directly at *me*) that only a "tiny, tiny minority" of postadolescent students will ever achieve near-native proficiency in a foreign language, and *none* will attain native proficiency. Long goes on to report in a matter-of-fact tone that the dimmest child will become far more proficient in his first language than the smartest adult in his second.

And I'm not even the smartest adult.

When Long opens the floor to questions, a woman strides purposefully to the microphone. Speaking in crisp British English, she demands to know why the success stories of thousands of adults in India who have successfully acquired near-native English proficiency (a definition that includes speaking without an accent) is not written about.

Long replies with a lengthy, academic answer involving studies of young women in third-world tribal areas who, when married into other tribes, reportedly picked up the language of their new tribe with ease—studies that, if confirmed, would make a mockery of all the perceived knowledge about second-language acquisition. "Yet when we looked into this reported phenomenon, there was no empirical data," Long says. "It was all subjective interpretation by the observers. So while I am sympathetic to your question, I have to say we need hard data before we can report on it."

This very *un*sympathetic reply infuriates the woman, who, while the rest of us heard "*Blah blah* research *blah blah* data," heard "Liar!"

"Well, I can tell you for a fact that this is happening," she shouts. "*I* am the data! I am one of these people! Yet as far as you are concerned, I don't exist!"

And I thought this conference was going to be dull. Although it never again approaches the emotional drama of the introductory session. Many of the talks I sit through over the next two and a half days, featuring such topics as "Transfer Effects in the L2 Processing of Temporal Reference" and "Using Prosodic Information to Predict Sentence Length," are Greek to me. This is mainly owing to my unfamiliarity with the subject matter, but the difficulty is compounded by the fact that the speakers are given only twenty minutes to present forty minutes of material, meaning that they all race through their PowerPoint slides, speaking at twice the rate of normal speech. This, I comment to a young Chinese graduate student during a break, seems a touch ironic, considering that this is a gathering of linguists, who should know better. She says, "Ironic? What does that mean?"

"Well," I say, knowing I'm in trouble, "for example, it's ironic that at a second-language acquisition conference you've asked me to explain a word that nearly all native speakers understand but that is nearly impossible to define. Isn't that one of the core problems for the second-language learner?"

Her brow furrows and she squints at my name tag. "Where do you teach?"

"Oh, I'm not a teacher. I'm an IT director at a psychiatric research institute."

This piques her interest. "You're doing psychiatric research on language acquisition?"

"No. I'm learning French."

I excuse myself and rush off to wolf down a muffin (better not attempt a word-for-word translation of *that* phrase into any language) on the way to the next session, where I hear that not only does the ability to acquire a second language become greatly diminished after adolescence, but the degradation continues linearly. That is, with each year, each *decade,* that I didn't get around to learning French, the goalposts have moved further away. What was once a relatively easy fifteen-year field goal has become fifty-seven-nigh-going-on-fifty-eight years, even by NFL standards a long kick. If I had known this forty years ago, had realized back then that I was in a virtual now-or-never situation, would I have moved up the priority of this task? Attempted the kick before losing more yardage?

More bad news: I learn that I will always have a strong accent because any second language I acquire will be filtered through the matrix of my first. The presenters themselves, nearly all foreign born, often struggle with English during their talks, and I find myself thinking, Jeez, if the experts are having this much trouble, things don't look good for me. I discover, to my great surprise, that Finns who move to Sweden at the age of *three* never attain native proficiency. Finns and Swedes? Don't they already speak nearly the same umlaut-laden language? *

This conference is looking like the worst pregame pep talk ever, the coach in the locker room warning, "Truth is, these guys are bigger and faster and smarter than we are, so forget winning; just try not to get hurt, boys." Until, that is, I sit down to lunch with Vince Lombardi—actually Heidi Byrnes, a professor of German at Georgetown University and president of the American Association for Applied Linguistics. It soon becomes clear that I've come to the right woman.

I know this because she opens the conversation by telling me I've come to the right woman. The feisty sixty-six-year-old, with a bit of the rebel in her, tells me not to listen to all the naysayers present. "The general trope out there is, hey, by the time you're fifteen or sixteen or seventeen, it's over. I just don't buy it—at all. It may be over, quote, unquote, whatever that means, for your phonetic features perhaps, but then you have to ask yourself, is that really the most important thing, that I am so completely indistinguishable as far as my accent is concerned? I don't think so."

---

* In what may portend my woeful linguistic instincts, it turns out that umlauts are about all that Finns and Swedes have in common. And reindeer.

The speakers do seem overly focused on this issue, yet even in the United States, a New Yorker sounds very different from a Californian. Furthermore, I point out, I love a woman with a French accent. If the actress Audrey Tautou spoke English *without* her gorgeous accent, she probably wouldn't be a star here.

"There you go," Byrnes agrees. "And yet, as we heard one more time today, that is an absolutely critical aspect of whether or not you 'pass.'"

Perhaps the picture isn't so bleak after all. As Byrnes and I continue discussing this gathering of professors and students of applied linguistics, I tell her I'm surprised by the highly theoretical nature of the presentations. I've found little here to guide me in my mission. "Excuse my naïveté," I say, trying not to sound too snarky, "but I thought *applied linguistics* meant that at some point, we were going to apply it."

Byrnes speaks with animation, but slowly, drawing out the occasional word for emphasis while adding meaning to her spoken words with her expressive hands—rubbing them together, pulling them apart, occasionally punctuating it all with a rich, hearty laugh. German-born, she is completely fluent in English, with traces of an accent—not German—that's hard to place, more regional American, perhaps, than foreign. "You have a field of applied linguistics that over the last thirty years or so found it necessary to establish its scientific credentials. And the way to do that was by very strong theorizing."

That's all well and good, and having spent most of my adult

life working in a research institute, I'm all for basic science, but, I wonder aloud, has all this theorizing and research (for example, tracking the eye movements of subjects as foreign words flash on a screen) yielded any practical results? "It seems to me we have a huge problem in this country," I say. "I have a friend—a very sharp guy—who studied French from the fourth grade through his sophomore year in college. Eleven years of French. And he goes to Paris and finds out he can't speak or even understand French. And this is not an uncommon story." Byrnes nods vigorously. "Isn't this a huge indictment of the state of language instruction in this country? This conference is in its third decade. After all this talk, all these papers and posters, after thirty years, have we made *any* progress in teaching foreign language?"

Byrnes tells me about the program they've developed in the Georgetown University German Department, where, by teaching German in a fashion in which "content learning and language learning can occur simultaneously"—in which every class attempts to connect the *learning* of a language with what you are going to be *doing* with the language—they have students coming in not knowing a word of German who are able to enroll in a German university after just four semesters.

Of course, Byrnes is speaking of eighteen- and nineteen-year-olds with their nimble brains. I ask her, "If you had me, not at eighteen, but now, at fifty-seven, when I can't even remember where I put the car keys—" She doesn't let me finish.

"I could do it!"

I feel like Eliza Doolittle talking to Henry Higgins.

"Really?"

"Absolutely! Because instead of thinking of you as a *deficit* learner—and you heard that, too, today, you're a deficit critter because you're past fifteen or past puberty—well, we're not going to dwell on that. We're not going to change that; that's a *birth phenomenon*."

I like that phrase. I'm not old, merely experiencing a "birth phenomenon."

Instead of letting my age handicap me, Byrnes says, she would build on it. "Instead, I'm going to say, he's a reasonably intelligent adult; let me take the cognitive abilities, the literate abilities, the interest that he has, and use those, and say, can I do something with them?—*precisely* because I know an adult learner is different from a child learner. So, rather than look at you as a deficit critter, I'll say, look what he can bring to the enterprise."

What can he—I—bring to the enterprise? My relative mastery of my first language, for one thing; I already know how language works. My maturity, for another. "You have enough of a sense of yourself, in contrast with some of our eighteen- or nineteen-year-olds, where this is a serious issue. They still are working on their identity. You *know* who you are."

Last time I checked—about four hours ago—I was a fifty-seven-year-old laughing at the Three Stooges on the hotel TV, but best not to bring that up. She tells me that students who go abroad for an immersion program are often afraid to speak, for fear of embarrassing themselves. "But you see, for me," Byrnes says, "I say, hey, what if they think, Gosh, she's stupid, why does she sound like this? That's not going to deeply affect my inner core of who I think I am; I can actually deal with that for the next five weeks. I can get something out of this. And I think you could, too."

I'm almost convinced, but not quite. "I know that at my age, I could learn woodworking, I could learn some math. But French?"

"You have swallowed what is the cultural trope: 'Just forget it, it's a hopeless undertaking, you don't have the memory, you can't remember the silly words, it's too complicated, all these dumb endings and pronunciation.' No, no, no!"

Heidi Byrnes is my ray of hope in a storm of second-language gloom, so enthusiastic, so utterly convincing, that I feel like I've climbed the mountain and reached the oracle. I ask the big question, the one that has brought me to this conference: "How do I proceed? How do I learn French?"

She sighs, and I feel the air deflating from me. "The difficulty you're going to have is you will essentially find no materials out there."

There are a number of self-instruction products available, I point out, not mentioning by name a certain yellow box that has been sitting on my desk, unopened, for three months.

"Yes, but you see, for reasons that make a lot of sense, they have to go on the behaviorist approach, what they call communicative language teaching. Every one of them markets themselves like that. 'We teach communication, and you will hear native speakers, situations in which you will learn how to function.'"

That actually doesn't sound so bad to me, and Byrnes acknowledges, "There's a lot to be said for that, for that will in fact enable you to do those sorts of things. By the same token, for us as an academic program, that kind of approach actually creates its own flat feeling because you come to see language and language learning in this purely instrumental way."

I've heard enough presenters here to realize that they all consider learning a language from computer software comparable to learning the guitar from Guitar Hero, a bias you might expect from academics. Thus I take Byrnes's warning with a grain of postgraduate salt and instead focus on the positive as she rushes off to attend the next session. *I am not a deficit learner. I don't feel foolish when I screw up. I am a confident adult, and most of all, I know who I am.*

Don't I?

First-Person Shooter

Man invented language to satisfy his deep need to complain.

—LILY TOMLIN

I make my way silently through thick undergrowth, part the vegetation, and spy my target: a young couple camping in the woods, alone. Or so they think. I edge closer. They hear a rustle and, surprised, look up at the intruder. My heart quickens.

"*Bonjour!*" I say into my microphone. "*Je m'appelle Bill.*"

"*Bonjour!*" they reply on the next slide.

Welcome to Rosetta Stone, the world's most popular language-learning software, whose ubiquitous yellow boxes are a familiar sight in airports, shopping mall kiosks, bookstores, and 2 a.m. infomercials. The reward for reaching the end of each unit, for having endured hours of dreary four-panel screens of very un-French photographs (all their language courses, from

Farsi to French, use the same set of photos), is a slide-show vignette that thrusts you into situations where you "engage" with the characters in the story. The idea is a noble one; after all, this is why you're learning a foreign language—to interact with people—and to drive home the point, Rosetta Stone shoots all these photographs from your perspective.

Unfortunately the resulting effect is less "you are there" than "first-person-shooter video game."

This initial vignette is utterly creepy. Are the Rosetta Stone developers unaware that they are closely mimicking a scene from every teenage slasher movie ever made? It's just bizarre. Continuing the stalker theme, the next vignette casts me as a young man picking up an attractive woman on a bus. Seriously. If this sounds vaguely familiar, it's because it resumes where the Rosetta Stone ads leave off, their message being that language class is really just a huge singles bar, which is how, at the end of unit 3, I find myself at a we-are-the-world party full of beautiful people of so many ethnic persuasions it rivals the famous *Star Wars* cantina scene. Of course, I don't know a soul and—worst of all—can't make any conversation because (and I grant that this is a backhanded compliment to Rosetta Stone) the first-person-shooter realism of this uncomfortable scene has locked out every word of French I've learned!

This is absolutely confidence-shredding, and as I stand there, my hand extended for a greeting with the charming hostess while she waits for me to say my lines, all I can think of is that this is *exactly* what's going to happen when I go to France in just a few weeks, that I will forget everything under pressure, and stammer and sweat and make a complete ass of myself. What are they expecting me to say here? Give me a clue!

Clues are few and far between. Because this is an immersion course, with no English explanations or translations, I sometimes find myself spending as much time trying to figure out what they want as learning French. Right now, it's taking me so long to come up with something that a message pops up asking if the microphone is working. Okay, okay! I try to focus on the dialogue, my sweaty virtual hand still extended in the camera frame while the woman, a smile frozen on her face, patiently waits for me to say something and consummate the greeting.

Just then, Anne walks in and sees the screen.

"Am I interrupting something?"

"I'm afraid not."

"I was just looking at the itinerary. Are we allowing enough time to catch the train to Normandy?"

Being a physician who needs to keep upwards of twenty appointments a day, my wife is, shall we say, attuned to scheduling, whereas I am attuned to efficiency, meaning I'm averse to waiting. "*Pas de problème,*" I say. "*La . . . la gare est . . . est*"—below, how do you say "below"? I had this a few weeks ago, "above" and "below," which are maddeningly similar, but that was, well, a few weeks ago. The hell with it. "Not to worry. The train station's right below the airport."

The question Anne ought to be asking is, have I learned enough in just three months of self-study to see us through ten days of biking in the French countryside, a trip we'd planned a year ago. I shouldn't have let Rosetta Stone gather dust on my desk all spring. It's been just . . . I don't know . . . *hard* . . . to begin. Before tackling French I wanted to acquire some cultural insight into the people who speak the language—I guess you could call it Georgetown's gestalt approach without the language part—so I set for myself a course prerequisite: *La Belle France,* Alistair Horne's history of the country, which runs a whopping five hundred pages, although it feels not a page over a thousand. Then I tackled an excellent book on the history of the French language, got inexplicably waylaid with research into the actual Rosetta Stone,* and spent weeks investigating (and buying) other language software, which also sits unopened but will be ready when I am. And of course there was the SLRF conference, the planning beforehand and the recuperation afterward.

It was, all in all, far more entertaining and less stressful *thinking* about learning French than actually learning French. And honestly, there seemed to be no rush. The Foreign Service

---

* The upshot: Inscribed in 196 BC, this famous stone, which, as we all learned in school, "unlocked the secrets of hieroglyphics," is not a prayer to the gods or soaring verse, but the utterly mundane decree of a tax exemption (in three languages) for the temples, demonstrating that then, as now, nothing wins votes like a tax cut.

Institute of the US State Department estimates that an English-speaking adult can achieve "basic fluency" in French with 480 hours of study. I've done the math: If I continue studying 2 hours a day, six days a week, I'll be "basically fluent" in a mere ten months. Or less. Having had a few years of French in high school, I have a bit of a head start. In fact, just before cracking open Rosetta Stone, I'd taken an online college-placement exam to see where I stand, and while I didn't do well enough for entrance into first-year college French, I missed by only a horse (*cheval*)—I mean, a hair (*cheveu*). A mistake anyone could make.

The results from another test, however, are far less reassuring. Georgetown linguist Heidi Byrnes had cautioned me against swallowing the "cultural trope" that we baby boomers don't have the memory to learn a language. Well, I thought, let's put that one to bed. So I took a computerized cognitive-assessment evaluation recommended by a colleague. I should've let sleeping dogs lie, for my memory score placed me in *the lowest 10 percent* of my age group. Put another way, 90 out of 100 fifty-seven-year-olds have better memory skills than I do. Baby boomer? I'm a baby bust! And this doesn't bode well for learning a new language, since what is language, after all, if not the ability to recall words and assemble them into meaningful structures?

Speaking of structures, another bright idea of mine wedged me inside one that I'm not looking forward to revisiting. Inspired by the fact that I work in a psychiatric research institute,

I thought it might be interesting to take functional MRI (fMRI) images of my brain while listening to French *before* I started studying the language and again after I'd learned it, six or ten or however many months from now, to see whether there was any indication, on a neurological level, of language acquisition, particularly in the areas of the brain associated with language. I'd feared I might be laughed out of the building when I approached the director of the institute's imaging center with my armchair science, but Dave Guilfoyle, who holds a PhD in physics, thought the experiment interesting enough to indulge me, scheduling time in the unit when it was idle and developing a protocol to detect the effect of French on my brain.

I can tell you right now the effect that merely being inside the fMRI scanner had on my brain: claustrophobia. I found myself fighting to remain calm inside the coffin-size tunnel of the machine, the *pow! pow! pow!* of the electromagnetic pulses so surprisingly loud that I felt like I was inside a jackhammer. Unable to move my arms, lift my head, or scratch my nose, my head encased in something resembling a high-tech football helmet, my right hand clutching the panic button, I took a couple of deep breaths as the first recording started playing through the headphones. Guilfoyle's protocol consisted of several short clips of, in turn, English, French, and Japanese, with brief resting intervals in between, in order to give us three composite brain images to compare later: my brain while listening to my native language, to the language I would be studying, and to a language that is and would remain totally foreign to me—and let's hope there's only one of those.

Which brings us back to Rosetta Stone Français, the first of several language-learning strategies I plan to employ. Having finally unwrapped the yellow box, I've been playing a fairly good catch-up game, running through it at more than twice the recommended pace of thirty minutes a day, then listening to the accompanying CD during my commute to work, followed by a French instructional podcast that I take along on my lunchtime walk—a solid two to three hours a day of French. Yet here I am, speechless at the door of my hostess as the program, baffled by my silence, again asks if my microphone is working. What on earth does it want me to say to this woman? How do I gain admission to this party?

Anne, satisfied with the travel arrangements to Normandy, heads out of the room, pausing at the door just long enough to look back over her shoulder and say breezily, "Try *bonsoir*."

And she doesn't even speak French.

William the Tourist
Meets William the Conqueror

A language is a dialect with an army and a navy.
—Yiddish linguist MAX WEINREICH

Surely *le conducteur* sees us running with our suitcases across the empty platform and will hold the doors another five seconds. *Juste cinq secondes!* But the doors slide closed just as I reach them, Anne trailing a few feet behind. After all, this is France, where keeping the trains on time is an obsession on a par with cheese.

But I'm from New York, where catching the subway is an obsession on a par with bagels, and with instincts honed from years of boarding the Broadway express, I reflexively (and recklessly, considering I'm on the eve of a ten-day bicycle trip) jam my knee into the rapidly closing gap. The doors hesitate, then briefly bounce open just long enough for Anne to slip in under my outstretched arm. Thankfully, improbably, we are aboard, sighing, then giggling with relief, until our fun is spoiled by *le conducteur.*

"*Billets?*" he requests. In the mad dash to the train, we've had to neglect one slight detail: tickets. Which is why the first words I say on French soil, before I can even catch my breath, are "*J'ai une petite problème,*" a bad omen. And even worse French. *Problème* is a masculine noun, despite the fact that it ends in what is to my mind a feminine-looking *e*, so I have *un problème,* not *une problème,* and one that is *petit,* not *petite,* because the adjective must agree in gender as well, so I've gotten three of out my first four French words wrong.

All of this is moot because I should've avoided that phrase entirely. In trying to minimize this teensy problem of holding no tickets, I've done the converse, for this sentence means the opposite of its literal words. In French, saying there is *un petit problème* means there is *un grand problème.* To put this into an American context, picture your bookie approaching you in a dark underground parking garage in Hoboken with the greeting, "Hey, buddy, we got a little problem here," and you get the idea.

Safe to say, not a good start to speaking French in France. But it gets worse. With what little French I have learned thus far in three months of study, I feel just barely prepared to order a simple dinner or check into a hotel—not, however, to explain to a conductor that I've already paid for the tickets online with a credit card but did not have the time to pick them up at the kiosk because our flight was two hours late and it took forever to get the baggage and we just barely made the train and, yes, I should've listened to Anne, who warned me the connection was too tight. I do remember the word for "late," so I say *en retard* a lot, but even though Rosetta Stone has drilled me ad nauseam on trains, buses, and planes, for the life of me I can't remember the words for "flight," "plane," "run," or "I'll give you a ten spot to make this problem go away," and even if I could, putting these words together into anything that resembles a narrative is far beyond my ability. So in the end I have to buy a second pair of tickets, but Anne and I are just relieved to be on the train and heading to what promises to be six glorious days of early autumn biking in Normandy and Brittany, followed by four more in Provence.

It's coincidental but apropos that we've chosen Normandy as our first destination in France, for it's the Normans we have to thank (although I doubt the English would use that word) for the fact that even before tackling French I already knew a number of French words, in addition to *petit* and *problème*. How much of our vocabulary is shared with French? To get an idea, take a stroll through an English garden (*jardin*), where you may find a *fleur* in bloom, perhaps an *insecte perché* atop a *rose,* enjoying the soft *pétales. Attention!* Some of these *plantes* might be *dangereuses,* while others are quite *délicieuses.*

A quarter to a third of all English words come from French,

and good thing; otherwise, learning this language would be even harder than it is. Which brings us to the question, how did this similarity between the French and English come to be?

THE HISTORY OF LANGUAGE is largely the history of invasions and migrations, and this is certainly true in the case of French and English. The first known outsiders to inhabit ancient Gaul (approximately modern France plus Belgium, a slice of Germany, and northern Italy) were the Greeks, who began arriving on the French Riviera, the Côte d'Azur, by sea during the first millennium BC. Recognizing the potential for film festivals, topless beaches, and casinos, they established trading posts along the Mediterranean, bringing their language and their culture, and founding Marseille, the first city in France, in 600 BC. Being a seafaring people, they didn't stray too far from the coast, keeping their distance from the Celts, who began to appear in northern and central France in the fifth century BC, and who get credit for founding Paris. The Celts continued expanding southward, however, bringing *their* language (Celtic) and culture, and a clash with the Greeks seemed inevitable until a far more powerful and threatening enemy appeared from the east: the Roman Empire.

The overmatched Celts, whom the Romans referred to as Gauls, fought the good fight for 150 years, and it took no less than Julius Caesar to finally subjugate them around 50 BC. It is estimated that over a million people—one out of every five

Gauls—were killed by the time Caesar declared, "All of Gaul is divided into three parts." Caesar made that statement in Latin, naturally, and as Roman magistrates, engineers, and other Latin speakers spread throughout the Roman province of Gaul, the conquered quickly adopted the conquerors' language. Latin was suddenly a prerequisite to getting ahead in life, whether you wanted the bread contract for a company of Roman soldiers or a job building an aqueduct. This was not the formal Latin of the orators, by the way, but common street Latin, known as Vulgar Latin, the Latin spoken by soldiers, merchants, and commoners. The French adoption of Latin is but one chapter in a story repeated again and again throughout history: the conquered learning the language of the conqueror (or sometimes vice versa), although it's likely that neither party really thought of their languages as different. Since there were no grammar texts or classes, the differences would have been seen simply as regional peculiarities, and languages often became mixed.

By AD 400 the Celtic tongue had vanished from Gaul altogether, but not without contributing its own unique flavor to Latin, which evolved into a dialect we call Gallo-Roman. A similar process was under way in the other reaches of the Roman Empire, producing, in addition to French, the Romance languages (so named because they are the languages brought by Rome)—Spanish, Italian, Portuguese, Romanian, and Catalan, to name the major ones.

In France, Gallo-Roman continued to evolve as new invaders

arrived, each group bringing a vocabulary indicative of its culture. The Vikings, or Norsemen (who became the Normans), contributed words related chiefly to naval affairs, while the migrating German tribes contributed over five hundred Teutonic words associated with the feudal system and hunting. Invaders, whether Vandals, Goths, Normans, Saxons, or Franks, tended to restrict themselves to distinct geographic regions, thereby creating their own versions of Gallo-Roman wherever they put down roots. Of these groups, the Franks, a loose collection of Germanic tribes originating on the east bank of the Rhône, played the largest role in the development of both France and French, contributing not only the first king of France, Clovis, but 10 percent of the words that survive today in modern French and the very name of the language itself: *français*.

By the tenth century there were dozens of different languages being spoken throughout France, but they can be categorized into just two major groups: those whose word for "yes" was a variant of the word *oïl* (the *langues d'oïl*) and those whose "yes" was a variant of the word *oc* (the *langues d'oc*). The *langues d'oïl* were spoken in the northern half of France; the *langues d'oc* in the south. Which would win out in the end? The growing influence of Paris boded well for *d'oïl,* but wandering troubadours spread the popularity of *d'oc* far and wide as they traveled through France, singing their popular tales of love and chivalry.

The similarity between English and French is a story not of love and chivalry but of war and treachery. The wheels were put into motion in the first week of 1066, when King Edward of England died without leaving an heir or naming a successor, throwing England into chaos. Well, politically at least. Most of the population couldn't have cared less. There's a great and not altogether implausible scene in *Monty Python and the Holy Grail* in which King Arthur rides up to a peasant woman (Terry Jones in drag) farming mud and announces haughtily, "I'm king of the Britons," to which the woman replies, "King of the *who*? Who are the Britons?" Arthur explains.

"I didn't know we had a king," she says.

Harold Godwinson, a powerful lord and son-in-law to King Edward, not only knew the Britons had a king, but thought the king was none other than himself. Claiming a deathbed anointment (unfortunately there were no witnesses), Harold had as good a claim to the throne as anyone and was named king by the commission of noblemen who had assembled in London to settle this mess. Meanwhile, news of King Edward's death had reached the not-so-distant shores of Normandy, a patchwork of duchies across the English Channel. A duke of one of those duchies, William (known at the time as Guillaume le Bâtard—William the Bastard—because of the illegitimacy of his birth), saw an opportunity to claim the throne for himself through a nebulous blood claim: his great-aunt was related to Edward's ancestors.

William was furious when he heard that Harold had ascended to the throne, for William's distinct recollection was that he had been promised the throne some years earlier by none other than Harold himself, back when they were best friends forever (possibly under duress, but a promise is a promise).

Harold retorted that he didn't remember saying any such thing, and even if he did say it, he didn't mean it, and even if he did mean it, he had no legal right to make such a promise. William in turn replied by assembling a large invasion force and building boats, lots of boats. Harold, having gotten wind of the sudden demand for oak in Normandy, hunkered down on the southwest coast of England with his army and waited. And waited. And waited. Across the channel, William was also waiting—waiting for favorable winds, because the sailing vessels of the day could sail only with the wind.

We'll leave William the Bastard waiting there for a bit, because as William the Tourist and his Duchess Anne are about to learn, you can wait a long time for the weather in Normandy to improve. I first feel the skies darken when Anne, settled on the train, picks up a discarded copy of *Le Figaro* and, frowning, asks, "What's the word for 'storm'?"

"DO YOU THINK," I yell through the wind to Anne as we bicycle toward the Normandy coast, our faces becoming reddened and sore from the pelting rain blowing directly in from the direction of England, "a nor'easter on this side of the Atlantic is a nor'wester?" The storm answers by literally blowing Anne and her bike to the ground. Yet not even the weather can prevent this from being a magnificent ride, through pastoral meadows and salt marshes filled with the bleating sheep who will provide tonight's dinner—the regional specialty known as *agneau de pré-salé,* salt-marsh lamb, which needs no seasoning because the meat is naturally salted from the marshland diet of the sheep. We often ride for miles without seeing a car or another human being, although Anne suggests that this may be because the weatherman has told everyone to stay indoors until this dangerous *typhon* blows over. Two hours into our ride, we round a corner and are so stunned by the apparition before us that we almost collide. "Camelot!" I cry, to the fanfare of imaginary trumpets.

"Camelot!" Anne cries as we stop alongside some curious cows.

"Eh, it's only a model!" I say in my best British accent, invoking yet another *Monty Python and the Holy Grail* line that never fails to get a laugh out of Anne—or me.

"Camelot" is actually Mont Saint-Michel. Built as a fortress, but today housing a monastery, it rises in the mist from the flat Normandy coast so suddenly and dramatically it seems as if the earth itself has thrust it upward, breathtaking, inspiring, almost hallucinatory in the fog, and, most importantly, our lunchtime destination. We pick up the pace, and during periods when the downpour eases enough for me to open my mouth without drowning, I lead spirited choruses of Mister Rogers's theme song: "It's a beautiful day in this neighborhood . . ."

Then we get lost, so lost that we don't even know whose neighborhood we're in. The directions provided by our out-fitter, who has supplied bikes and who transports our luggage inn-to-inn for this self-guided bike tour, are precise when least needed and vague at the most critical junctions, resulting in long stretches of staring at maps in the driving rain. Dis-oriented and out of ideas, we stop at a café to ask for directions, and while the men inside try to be helpful as we stand there with our Michelin map, water dripping onto their floor, they seem to view the map as a novelty; in fact, it seems as if it's the first time they have ever seen a map of their own region. France invented the road map, for God's sake! (Michelin, the tire company, got into the map and restaurant-guide business as a way to encourage people to drive into the country, thus wearing out their Michelin tires sooner.) The locals can't make any more sense of the directions or the map than we, but in the end their local knowledge of the area gets us back on track and we finally reach the fortress.

And what a fortress. The massive stone structure, begun in medieval times and rebuilt and enlarged throughout the cen-turies, sits on a tiny island that is accessible from the mainland via a sandbar when the tide is low, and protected from invaders and infidels when it is not. As the difference between low and high tide can be as much as forty-six feet (!), more than one sol-dier (or tourist, and that's no joke) has drowned by mistiming the crossing. The famous Bayeux Tapestry, which illustrates the story of the Norman invasion, depicts Harold Godwinson (not yet King Harold) rescuing two of William's Norman knights from the tidal flats back in happier days.

The contemporary visitor need not risk his life to visit the abbey; today the island can be reached safely via a causeway and a car park. It is, I will warn you, a touristy, touristy place—the French seem no better at avoiding that fate than Americans—but to a pair of wet bicyclists the citadel offers comforting fish soup and a welcome break from bicycle seats and rain. After a tour, before remounting the bikes, we score some plastic bags to put between our shoes and socks from a friendly shopkeeper, because I remember the word *sac* and I fake (correctly, as it turns out) "plas-teek."

Two more phrases I know: *il pleut* (it's raining) and *il pleure* (he's crying), although I tend to mix them up. I remember them because of what, I explain to Anne between raindrops, is the poetry of it, rain as nature's tears. Or vice versa. *Il pleut* plenty and we're so tired we're on the verge of *pleure* when we finally reach our destination, the town of Pontorson. As we pedal past a bus stop, a young woman who's just gotten off a bus asks us for directions to the train station.

"*Là-bas,*" Anne says, before I can answer. "*À gauche.*"

"*Merci.*"

"*De rien. Au revoir!*"

I could not have been more shocked if my bicycle started talking. "Two questions," I say. "We don't know where *we're* going. How can you give her directions?" Anne shrugs. "And when did you learn French?"

"I've just picked a little up along the way."

Not from me she hasn't. I don't know whether to laugh, cry, or rain.

I IMAGINE NEITHER DID my namesake, William the Bastard (that's namesake as in "William," not as in "Bastard"), in August and September of 1066 as he waited in vain, week after week, for the contrary Normandy winds to shift. Across the channel in England, King Harold, growing equally frustrated with the wait, decided finally that if William hadn't come by now, he wasn't coming—surely, no one in his right mind would start a war on foreign soil as winter approached. So Harold disbanded his restless army to allow the men to get back to their fields in time for the fall harvest. That was on September 8. On September 27 the wind direction shifted to the south and William set sail for the coast of southern England with 696 ships. Meanwhile, nearly simultaneously, yet another claimant to the throne, the Norwegian king Harald III, had landed in York, in the northern part of England, with fifteen thousand men, one of whom was Harold's estranged brother. (This kind of intrigue demonstrates why Shakespeare was able to make a living off writing historical plays.)

King Harold-with-an-*o* quickly reassembled his force and rushed to York to defeat to the death King Harald-with-an-*a* and Harold's no-good brother in a furious battle, and the victorious troops were just catching their breaths and celebrating when a courier arrived with the news that William had landed on the undefended southwest coast of England, which he was undoubtedly surprised to find deserted. Harold raced south with his exhausted forces in one of the great marches in military history, but William had already gained a crucial foothold. Harold's tired and weakened troops were defeated, and Harold was killed in the Battle of Hastings. William continued his brutal conquest of England—he was by all accounts not a gentle man—and on Christmas Day, 1066, just shy of a year since King Edward's death, William the Conqueror (né William the Bastard), a Frenchman, was crowned king of England.

The Normans made French the official language of England, bringing it first to the English royal court, then beyond, to the schools, courts, and commerce, as the tongue evolved into Anglo-Norman, which was French with an English twist. A thousand years later, some of our legal terms betray this uneasy Anglo-French alliance. Ever wonder why a court orders you to redundantly "cease *and* desist"? Aren't those two words synonyms? They are, but the English word "cease" was coupled with the official French verb *desister* to make sure everyone knew what the court was talking about. Same for "null and void."

England wouldn't be ruled by a king whose native tongue was English until 1399, an astounding three centuries later, when

King Henry IV took the throne. The English that Henry spoke, though, would be far changed from the Old English in use before the Norman invasion. As we know, countless French words had by then become part of Standard English. Some of these, such as *plege* and *remaindere,* are no longer used in French, although their English forms persist. Others, while we understand them, are used only in formal English. We might *commence* firing, but we begin everything else.

It can be revealing to look at the origins of some of our French-derived words. Millions of Americans finding their homes being foreclosed might be interested to know that "mortgage" literally means "death contract." Another favorite of mine is "curfew," which comes from the French *couvre-feu,* the time when everyone must cover his fire. At the same time, some, but not nearly as many, English words made it into French (including, rather ironically, considering how this whole thing started, "boat," which returned across the English Channel to become *bateau*).

ANNE AND I COULD use a *bateau* on the second day of our trip as we cross from Normandy into Brittany in the pouring rain, looking for a place to have lunch, which is more difficult than we'd expected, for the small, picturesque villages the route takes us through are often so small that they don't even have a restaurant, only a *boulangerie* and sometimes a *charcuterie,* which sells cold meats such as sausages and pâtés.

Together these would make a fine lunch—except that all the shops close down at lunchtime, including the ones that sell food. I wonder how long my local deli would survive if it closed every day for lunch. But at a small, nearly deserted café in a small, nearly deserted village somewhere in Brittany—we're not exactly sure where—the proprietor takes pity on us, and even though they serve food only on weekends, at the urging of one of the regulars he warms up some soup. I don't know where this notion of the French being rude comes from. Probably from rude Americans. Only a few days into our trip, young men have helped us put air in our tires with the unfathomable French pump supplied with the bikes, a shopkeeper has given us bags for our feet, a café owner who doesn't serve lunch has prepared us lunch, and everyone has been eager to give us directions, which is giving me a chance to practice my French, although what I mainly practice saying is *nous sommes perdus*—we're lost.

Sure enough, after lunch we are *perdus* once again, although at least the rain has stopped for a bit. "Let me ask this man getting his mail," I say to Anne as we brake to a stop. He looks like a classic French pensioner, with his shot-glass-thick glasses and walking cane, a man with all the time in the world to help us find our way.

"Billy, I don't think he's—" Anne starts to protest, but too late. I am confident, in the mood to speak French, and off.

"*Excusez-moi, monsieur,*" I say with a smile. "*Bonjour! Nous sommes perdus.*"

He asks where we are going. Dinan, I tell him.

"*Ah, bon?*" We must be on the right track.

I show him the map and point to a spot. "*Est-ce que nous sommes ici?*" Are we here? As with the previous men, he seems never to have seen a map of his own neighborhood. I point to the road I think we're on and ask if we're here, on the D34. He frowns, consults the map, flips it top to bottom, and points to an entirely different spot. "*Non, non, nous sommes ici.*"

I give the news to Anne, who expresses grave doubt. "He lives here," I argue. "He ought to know." Twenty minutes and a few miles later, it becomes clear that he doesn't know. And that I don't know that *Ah, bon?* when inflected as a question means not "Oh, good" but (as with *j'ai un petit problème*) the opposite: "Oh, really? (That's what you think!)"

"I can't figure out the French," I fume to Anne as we back-track in the rain, adding yet more precious miles to the already long day. "How can they not know the name of the road they live on?"

"Well, maybe next time you might not want to ask a blind man." Oh, *that's* why she was trying to stop me.

We reach the walled medieval city of Dinan, built high on a hilltop in order to defeat foreign invaders and tired cyclists, long after dark, having traveled some fifty miles, by far the longest (and wettest) bike trip we've ever done in our lives, but the French penchant for dining late plays to our favor, our reward for the long day being a memorable meal in a cozy and dry seventeenth-century inn.

The next morning we are back in the wet saddles for several

more days of riding in the rain, but the sun finally breaks through as we return to the Brittany coast, riding past half-timbered cottages and atop seaside cliffs, the waves crashing below. Biking is a wonderful way to see a country. True, in a car you could cover ten times the distance as on bikes, but while you might see more, you wouldn't see as much. Zooming by at forty or sixty miles an hour, even if you traveled the back roads we are traversing, which would be unlikely, you might glimpse the cottages but not notice the gardens or where new construction has almost seamlessly joined old. You might've seen the ducks in the yards but would've missed the old woman coming out and grabbing one by the neck.

We roll into the final stop of the trip, the seaside resort town of Dinard (not to be confused with nearby Dinan), which is somewhat incongruously overseen by a larger-than-life statue of a famous Brit, Alfred Hitchcock. Local legend has it that Hitchcock based the spooky house in *Psycho* on one he saw in Dinard, giving the town a convenient excuse for an annual film festival that brings in millions of euros. At the hotel, my rehearsed, once-memorized sentence asking where we should store the bicycles is nowhere to be found, and I fumble with some inadequate replacement phrases before it finally comes to mind. Yet even then, it turns out to be useless, because my pronunciation is so bad as to render my French unintelligible. Finally I just shrug and ask, "*Les vélos?*"

The clerk has us follow her outside, where she tries to tell us something of apparent great importance, without success. She says something, I say something in return, she shakes her head and says something else. This goes on for several minutes, both of us growing increasingly exasperated—wait a minute, I don't have to describe the scene; it's a virtual replay of the one in *The Return of the Pink Panther* where Peter Sellers's Inspector Clouseau is trying to check into a hotel, his preposterous French accent (*I* should talk . . .) pulling the *r* in "room" from somewhere between his larynx and his liver.

CLOUSEAU: Do you have a rgghum?

CLERK: A . . . "rgghum"?

CLOUSEAU: What?

CLERK: You said, do I have a "rgghum"?

CLOUSEAU [IMPATIENTLY]: I know perfectly well what I said; I said, do you have a rgghum!

CLERK: You mean, do I have a *room*.

CLOUSEAU: That is what I have been saying, you fool!

This fool is saved by Anne, who finally figures out from the clerk's sign language that she is asking if we have a lock for the bikes. Like Clouseau, my greatest challenge is the French *r*. In English, we pronounce words with a leading syllabic *r*—"ready," "arrive," and, of course, "room"—with what is called the alveolar approximant, with the tip of the tongue slightly rolled back, safely out of the way, while the teeth touch lightly on the lower lip. In French, however, the *r* sound is produced using the uvular rhotic, a guttural sound that is produced by placing the back of the tongue firmly against the back of your throat with an open mouth, the result being a sound so different from our *r* that it ought to be represented by a different letter of the alphabet.

Anyway, my Clouseau impersonation over, we lock up the bikes, take turns soaking in the tub, and then head out for a walk and a drink. Speaking of movies, we've had the outfitter alter the standard tour to include this stop in Dinard solely because of the effect that Éric Rohmer's film *A Summer's Tale,* which was shot in Dinard, had on me years ago. It is your typical French movie, meaning that there's not much of a plot, but there are plenty of long, talky walks featuring teenagers in existential angst discussing the meaning of life; in this case the walks occur on the trails cut into the cliffs surrounding Dinard, and ever since seeing those dramatic paths I've wanted to vacation here with Anne. Go ahead and snicker, but yes, I have based our vacation on a few scenes from a fictional movie filmed thirty years ago.

It never rains in *A Summer's Tale,* but despite the sunshine we are enjoying now, the heaviest rain yet is forecast for tomorrow. Not a day for walking the trails, which we've been looking forward to for years. "Let's do them now," Anne says cheerily, and we spend what's left of the afternoon in our own Rohmer movie, except *our* existential crisis is how to escape the rain of Brittany.

Over drinks afterward we decide to bail out of Brittany a day early to head to sunny Provence, where we'll be biking the rest of our trip. This means checking the train schedule, contacting our tour coordinator, finding a room in Avignon, and so on. I'll need help, and I dread trying to relate all of this to the clerk, who doesn't speak a word of English.

"Maybe," I say to Anne as we devour a towering platter of chilled *fruits de mer*—literally, "fruits of [the] sea," the incredibly lovely French term for seafood—"someone else will be at the front desk when we return."

No such luck. I try to make a fresh start by apologizing for the earlier scene with the bikes, explaining my terrible French by saying that I am *très, très fatigué* from all the biking and rain. It seems I find myself saying "sorry" a lot in France, although only later do I realize that at least half the time I've been saying not *désolé*, but *désiré*, and you don't need your French dictionary to know the difference between those two words. This possibly Freudian slip might be what sends the young clerk, who bears a resemblance to the sexy French actress Ludivine Sagnier, over the edge.

"Would you prefer I speak English?" she says sweetly.

"Sure, if you don't mind—" What? *She speaks English?* Why on earth did she put me through that nonsense with the bike locks? Did she learn English in the past hour while I was eating oysters? This is a communication phenomenon we have already experienced more than once on this trip. So, regaining

my composure, I politely ask her why, given my obvious struggle and inability to communicate, and her fluency in English,
she let me continue stammering away in pidgin French.

"You need the practice," she says with a smile.

Touché.

ARRIVING IN SUNNY, WARM Provence, we find a
timeless place of Roman ruins, fields of lavender, olive trees,
and cobblestone streets, alive with the ghosts of Van Gogh,
Cézanne, and Marcel Pagnol. And something else I hadn't expected: street signs in two languages: French and Occitan, the
language of southern France, the *langue d'oc*.

Remember that when William the Conqueror sailed for England, there were still two families of very different languages
being spoken in France—the *langues d'oïl* (those languages
spoken in the north of France, centered around Paris) and the
langues d'oc (those of the south, centered on Toulouse, in the
heart of southern France). It was becoming clear that sooner or
later there was going to be one France: which language would it
speak? Northern France had the might of Paris, the king of the
Franks, and the armies. Southern France had the troubadours
and Toulouse. Guess who won?

The day the music died arrived in 1209, when the troubadours, caught up in a bit of holy war not of their making, fled
mostly to Spain, while the king of the Franks saw a chance to
double the size of his kingdom, virtually destroying Toulouse

in the process. *D'oc* would not expand into northern France. Yet it wasn't going away quite yet. Despite efforts by Napoleon to make what was now known as French (the language derived from the *langues d'oïl*) the only language of France, even as late as World War I, many young men from "the provinces" heard French for the first time when they were conscripted into the army, for pockets of local languages and dialects still thrived in such areas as Provence, Brittany, and Alsace. The first words these men learned may have been "Ready . . . aim . . . fire!" but learn French they did. The *langues d'oc* today survive mainly as a regional dialect of French and in the form of these redundant street signs, a display of local pride, as well as in the name of a region—the Languedoc—that Peter Mayle made famous (some would say ruined as a result of its ensuing popularity) in his book *A Year in Provence*. Well, nothing can ruin our week in Provence. With new bikes, better directions, and much better weather, Anne and I set off on the short ride from Avignon to Saint-Rémy-de-Provence, once home to Vincent van Gogh. Saint-Rémy is your typical Provençal town, with narrow, winding streets; restaurants with outdoor seating ideal for people watching; fountains; a nice little church; and a street market.

What drew Vincent van Gogh here from Arles in 1889, however, was its asylum. While not wrestling his demons, Van Gogh was allowed outside the grounds, where he painted, in a single year, some of his best-known works: *The Starry Night, Bedroom in Arles,* and *The Sower,* to name a few. Van Gogh's Saint-Rémy period is characterized by the broad, energized, almost manic swirls of cypresses and, most famously, the stars of *The Starry Night*. It is a starry night, and Anne and I can't resist. After dinner we walk to the edge of town and look up. "Nope, same stars as at home," I say to Anne. "It was all in his mind." His poor, tortured, brilliant mind. But thank God for that mind.

While in Saint-Rémy, Van Gogh also painted *Olive Trees with the Alpilles in the Background*. It is a hallucinatory, even frightening painting, the olive trees twisting in agony toward the sky, reflecting the tormented state of the painter, the Alpilles Mountains roiling in the background like a stormy sea. Those menacing mountains, clearly visible in the starlight, lay between us and our next destination, the city most associated with Van Gogh: Arles.

Taking a slow but steady approach, Anne and I climb *les Alpilles* without too much difficulty, the scenery being so utterly beautiful we forget how hard we're working. The mountains, protected as a national park, covered with olive trees and almond groves, and breathing an intoxicating herbal scent I can't place, seem not to have changed much since Van Gogh's time. We pause at the summit to gaze at Arles, looking angular and Cézanney (and far) in the distance. Then with a push we are whooshing down the mountain, whooping with joy as we careen through switchbacks and lean into turns, flying past other bicyclists huffing and puffing their way up the mountain, descending toward the timeless city of Arles.

By late afternoon, we are watching the sun set from atop the Roman amphitheater. But it doesn't just set; in French it literally goes to bed. *Le soleil se couche.* As if you were saying your son is going to bed (*mon fils se couche*). In the morning, both your sun and your son *se lèvent.* In between, there is not just twilight, but the time *entre chien et loup*—between the dog and the wolf—the time when the light is so dim you can't distinguish a dog from a wolf, although this poetic idiom is also used to describe one who is between the familiar and the unknown, the comfortable and the dangerous, between the domestic and the wild.

That's how I often feel while in France, especially when our visit to Provence is cut short by a national strike (*la grève*) called for the day we are to return by train to Paris. Two million— not twenty thousand or even two hundred thousand, but *two million*—French workers and students take to the streets, protesting President Nicolas Sarkozy's proposed raising of the retirement age—to sixty-two.

On the last day of our bike trip, as we're preparing to return home, we finally meet the driver who's been transporting our bags from hotel to hotel each day while we bike, a classic working Frenchman with a firm handshake and a Gallic twinkle in his eye. He asks where we're from, and when we say the United States he nods gravely, smiles, and says, "*Courage!*" before taking his leave. Anne and I take it to be a reference to our country's wars in Iraq and Afghanistan, although for all we know he means much more. He might as well have been referring to my French. This trip has made it clear that I have a lot of work ahead of me. I'm going to have to buckle down, double up, get to it, if I am going to have any hope of learning French before fatigue and discouragement set in, leaving me roadkill on the route to Paris, just another statistic. Several of the French we've met during this trip tell us they've learned English as adults, making me wonder whether they have some secret, some technique that we're missing in the States.

Having lunch outdoors at a small café, I hear a vaguely familiar voice from, of all people, our French waiter, who speaks English with hardly a trace of a French accent. In fact, his English, if anything, suggests the eastern United States, where I've lived my entire life. He must have done some immersion study there.

I tell Anne, "I want to speak French the way he speaks English."

He brings us the check. "Your English is perfect," I say. "You've spent some time in the States, no?"

"Actually, I haven't."

"Really? How did you learn such good English?"

"Watching Jerry Seinfeld."

A Room with a *Veau*

· ·

He that travelleth into a country before he hath some entrance
into the language, goeth to school, and not to travel.

——FRANCIS BACON

Back home, I've returned to my routine of watching an hour
a day of TV5Monde, the international French-language cable
network that rebroadcasts programs from France and other
francophone countries. Anne wanders in from the kitchen.
"What are you watching?"

"A sitcom out of Quebec."

"Any good?"

"It's no *Seinfeld.*"

For that matter, it's no *Three's Company,* but I've been enduring it for one compelling reason, an oddity that Anne instantly
notes. "It's subtitled in French? Why? It's *in* French!"

"Not according to the French, it's not. It's their way of re-minding Canadians they don't really speak French." Although you could've fooled me; to my tin ear it sounds totally French, aside from a few Anglicisms thrown in here and there. But the superfluous French subtitles make a superuseful learning tool for the student of French. And right now I need all the tools I can get. Anne, however, isn't convinced of my new method.

"Aren't there any French classes around?"

The hairs on the back of my neck bristle. Classes are a sore point with me for a couple of reasons. Back before the richest country in the world decided to start behaving like one of the poorest, you could generally find an evening "adult ed" lan-guage class at your local high school or community college. Such programs are an endangered species today, and if you can find any language class at all, it's nearly always Spanish. Yet it wasn't that long ago that French was a language that all well-educated Americans spoke, the language of culture and diplomacy, to the extent that treaties were drafted in French even when neither country was a francophone nation. French-speaking Jacqueline Kennedy was adored as the very height of sophistication. By contrast, in recent years unsuccessful pres-idential aspirants John Kerry and Mitt Romney were both victims of political attack ads based on the accusation that they—gasp!—spoke, as the *New Yorker* recently called it, "the language that dare not speak its name," the implication being that they were socialist-sympathizing, snail-eating, effete pansy snobs living in the past, out of touch with the common joe.

Well, I have news for the political masterminds behind these ads: French is Rosetta Stone's second-best-selling foreign language (behind only Spanish) among the common joes of America. The official language of twenty-nine countries, it is spoken regularly by some 175 million people, not counting another 200 million occasional speakers and students. TV5Monde ranks behind only CNN and MTV in number of worldwide viewers, and France has the world's fifth-largest economy. So let's not count French out just yet. But all that doesn't make it any easier to find a French course in the Mid-Hudson Valley.

"The nearest night classes are in the city," I tell Anne. "That's a hundred-and-twenty-mile round-trip. For an eight o'clock class I'd be getting home at midnight. And I've tried weekly classes before. They just don't work. Do you know a single adult who's ever learned a language that way?"

Anne meekly raises her hand.

"That was *medical* Spanish. Doesn't count."

"*Sí, cuenta,*" she protests. Perhaps it does count, but Anne speaks the most curious flavor of Spanish you'll ever encounter. She can quite capably conduct a thirty-minute physical in Spanish, but put her in a Spanish restaurant and she can't read the menu unless they're serving stiff necks and joint pain.

The truth is, the reason for my avoidance of a French class

may lie less with geography than with psychology. Four decades later I'm still scarred from my classroom experience with . . . I dare not speak *her* name . . . Madame D——, my high school French teacher.

"Ma-*dame*," as we called her, was an imposing figure, sporting a prominent mole on one cheek that rooted a single, prominent hair, and a glare that could melt a wheel of Brie. Discipline was rarely a problem in her classroom (a classmate who acted up was once literally dragged out of the room by her ear), and every French class was a forty-five-minute sentence to the Bastille. Her cumulative years of teaching may have done more harm to Franco-American relations than freedom fries.

I'm sure there was more than one French teacher in the school district, but I always seemed to end up in Madame's class. This was almost certainly due to some behind-the-scenes maneuvering by my father, who was a guidance counselor in the junior high school and thought he was doing me a favor by making sure I had the "best" French teacher, having himself never been pulled out of Madame's class by the ear. This favoritism in turn made me a favorite of Madame's—meaning I was called on a lot—even though I was a poor French student. My occasional stutter, which remained mostly under the surface when answering math- or science-class questions, became amplified to King George VI proportions under the lethal combination of Madame's torture chamber and the inescapable fact that the main objective in this class was *to speak perfectly.*

No surprise, then, that I dropped French after my sophomore year, the moment I'd fulfilled the graduation requirement, to the consternation of my parents, who thought I might be torpedoing my college prospects. *Pas de problème:* I'd discovered that engineering programs, for which I was otherwise ill suited, generally didn't carry a language requirement. Which is how I ended up a biomedical engineering major. After a disastrous freshman year largely spent unsuccessfully trying to get a picture on the oscilloscope, the school of liberal arts discontinued its foreign language requirement (while keeping its swimming requirement), clearing the way for me to switch my major to English, to the visible relief of my engineering professors and classmates.

In other words, I chose a college major primarily on the basis of *not having to take French.* Then how on earth did I end up trying to make amends forty years later? How did my determination to avoid French become an equally strong determination to learn it? Let's pick up the story after college, in a tale I call

The Boy, the Girl, and the Cow;
or, A Little French Is a Dangerous Thing

In 1975, a year after graduating, jobless (thanks to my degree in English) and aimless but debt-free, as most college graduates were in those days, I bought an international youth hostel card and a student Eurail pass, stuffed a backpack, and spent the next several months traveling alone throughout Europe. My journey took me from Norway to Greece, a wonderful adventure when you're young and single and have no agenda or timetable. The title of a popular guidebook of the era was *Europe on $10 a Day*, and back then it was possible, particularly if you slept mostly at youth hostels.

Doing the hostel circuit, you tend to cross paths with people more than once, sometimes several countries and weeks apart, and you may even do a little traveling together, as solo travel can get lonely. Thus when I parted with Judy, a young Canadian whom I'd met in Norway and again by chance in Germany, we'd agreed to meet up once more in a few weeks to share a gustatory fantasy that it turned out we'd both secretly been harboring: one haute cuisine meal in a fine, white-tablecloth French restaurant before returning home. Judy and I had each saved up enough money for this by eating cheaply in cafeterias and sleeping on trains during our journeys.

Lyon made for a convenient rendezvous and, as one of the culinary centers of France, not a bad place at all to have our ultimate French dining experience. The stakes were high: three months of travel, just one chance, one splurge. Everything had to be perfect. We carefully selected the restaurant, made a reservation, and put on the best clothes we could dig out of our backpacks. For me that meant a ratty light brown corduroy jacket and shiny vinyl shoes (the first rainfall had washed the faux-leather coating off these lightweight, backpackable shoes); for Judy, a red-and-white checkered skirt that—she shrieked with horror when she put it on—made her look like a walking Italian tablecloth. Dressed for puttin' on the ritz, we headed out to dine at the very unfashionable hour of 7 p.m.

Things were going swimmingly until I opened the menu and realized that I'd left my pocket French-English dictionary back at the hostel. No matter; I figured I remembered enough French from high school to at least order dinner, and besides, I already knew what I wanted. My heart soared when I recognized *veau* on the menu. Although for some reason it was only served for two. "Come on, we've got to get this," I told Judy, repeating what I'd read in a guidebook. "Veal is a specialty of this region. The calves are milk-fed and killed very young. You can't get veal like this at home at any price."

"But what's this *rognons* part?" The full name of the dish was *rognons de veau*.

"I don't know. What's the difference? It's veal *something*. It probably describes the sauce or the way it's cooked. I'll ask the waiter."

Even at twenty-two I knew better than to ask a Frenchman— especially a French waiter—if he spoke English, which is considered rude and insulting. You should attempt to speak in French, no matter how bad your French might be, and hope you get a reply in English, but in this fancy restaurant, with the stakes high, the prices higher, and the mustachioed waiters straight out of central casting, my nerves got the better of me, and to Judy's alarm and mine alike, I blurted out, "Do you speak English?" The only explanation I have for the reaction that followed was that the poor non-English-speaking fellow must have thought I said, "Do you sodomize your mother?"

"Now you've done it," Judy said, half laughing after he'd brusquely left the table. "Nice work." Still, I was able to coax her into joining me in *rognons de veau* for two.

"Something else?" Central Casting had asked in French when I placed the order. "*Non, merci*," I replied. The veal was so expensive we decided to forgo an appetizer. He looked at us quizzically and marched off, I'm sure to have a good laugh in the kitchen, and a half hour later our *rognons de veau* arrived, looking very lonely on the plate.

"What's this?" Judy cried, looking down at a large white china plate that was completely bare save for a handful of what looked like deer droppings, little brown things the size of grapes, rolling around on the naked plate. No potatoes, no vegetable, not even a garnish. The waiter, in repayment for my blunder, had apparently elected not to explain that *à la carte* in this restaurant meant that the main course did not come with things like vegetables and potatoes; those needed to be ordered separately. Nothing but these mysterious, unappetizing droppings sitting starkly on the white china.

Judy gingerly poked a fork into one and tasted it. "Kidneys! You ordered me kidneys! The one thing in the world I can't stand!"

"That's impossible. The menu said *veau*. I know for a fact that *veau* is veal."

She set one rolling toward me with her fork as her eyes welled up. "My one splurge in Europe, and it's kidneys!"

The mystery was cleared up that evening when I retrieved my dictionary. *Veau* is indeed "veal"—I was right about that—but it also has another meaning in French: "calf." *Rognon,* as we knew all too well by then, is "kidney." Thus *rognons de veau* are literally "calf's kidneys." We Americans raise calves but eat veal, I suppose to gloss over the fact that we're eating a young animal that was adorably drinking milk from a baby's bottle a few days ago, while the French, who are far less squeamish about their food sources, matter-of-factly and merrily raise, slaughter, and then eat calf. This lack of differentiation between animal and meat applies to other species as well. In America we eat beef, never cows. In France both the meat and the steer are called *boeuf.* We eat pork, not pigs, while *cochon* and *porc* are interchangeably used for "pig" and "pork" alike.

After my veal error, things were never quite the same between Judy and me, two people whose relationship was fractured by a single translation error. The romance we might have been on the cusp of never developed, and we soon parted ways. Yet before I boarded the plane home, I'd be very much in love. With a country.

THE LOVE BUG MAY have bitten me in France, but the fever took root after I returned home. Living in New York City, I couldn't get enough of France. I discovered François Truffaut, then Éric Rohmer and other *auteurs* of the French New Wave cinema during joyful hours squinting at jumpy subtitles in mostly empty New York art-house theaters, as France revealed itself frame by frame in grainy black and white. I listened to French music, read Camus and Sartre.

I married and had kids, and when Zach and Katie were in their teens I took the family to Paris, and although I tried to retrieve some of that high school French, my attempts to speak the language resulted in largely unintelligible exchanges with taxi drivers and waiters, during which I would say things like, "It sleeps very cold in the soup."

After that first visit, I went back twice more with Anne, who by now was every bit as enchanted with France as I. Strolling the streets of Paris, we'd stop to look at the listings in real estate office windows and drool enviously over photographs of a Latin Quarter apartment or a Norman cottage, although they were far out of our financial reach. More realistically, we dreamt about vacations spent bicycling France's quiet country roads and canals, peddling alongside vineyards, farms, and streams. Yet we always felt like outsiders, like the tourists we were, because neither of us spoke the language, a decided disadvantage that became quite apparent when I took a week-long bread-making course, without English subtitles, at l'École Escoffier. I did experience my moment of linguistic glory, however, when Anne and I were sitting on a park bench after class one day and a Frenchman asked me, "*Quelle heure est-il, s'il vous plaît?*"

Asking the time happens to be a stock phrase, found in every guidebook, learned in every French course, so I knew what he was saying. But a response? I never really learned my numbers—even up to sixty—so almost certainly I was going to end up shrugging, shaking my head, or inelegantly sticking my wrist in his face to let him see for himself. But when I glanced down at my watch, I realized my extraordinary fortune. It was *exactly noon*. "*Il est midi,*" I said as coolly and fluently as a native. He thanked me, and I nodded and tossed off another stock phrase, "*De rien,*" don't mention it.

In my book, that qualified as a conversation, and this brief escape from the tourist's cocoon had me walking on air for the rest of the trip. Wouldn't it be wonderful to be able to do that all the time? Wouldn't it be nice to never again accidentally order organ meats? If so, I'd better dramatically improve my French. Maybe Anne was right; I did need to bury the ghost of Madame D—— and get into a classroom.

Your French Is Killing Me

. . . .

The French . . . always tangle up everything to that
degree that when you start into a sentence you never know
whether you are going to come out alive or not.

—MARK TWAIN

"*Quel âge avez-vous?*" the young instructor I'll call Mademoiselle D—— wants to know. I can see her grainy image in the
corner of the computer screen, but she can't see me. And good
thing, because the other question she might logically be asking
is, "Why are you sweating like a *cochon?*" having pretty much
covered "How stupid are you?" and "You're pulling my leg,
right?"

I *think* that's what she said, or something to that effect, but
no English is allowed in this online immersion class. It's as if
Madame D—— has managed to get reincarnated as a younger,

only slightly gentler version of herself in order to torment me once again. At least this time I'm not embarrassing myself in front of the other students. This is because I'm the only student who's signed up for this 7 a.m. lesson, a huge miscalculation on my part, and Mademoiselle seems none too pleased at having lost her lunch hour in France, where it's 1 p.m., to a clueless, middle-aged American who can't even state his age. I can't state my age partly because the pressure has made the word for "fifty" fly out of my head and partly because French has a numbering system that is only slightly less complicated than the Babylonian calendar. It reminds me of Alice's encounter with the queens in *Through the Looking-Glass:*

> "Can you do addition?" the White Queen asked. "What's one and one and one and one and one and one and one and one and one and one?"
>
> "I don't know," said Alice. "I lost count."
>
> "She can't do addition," the Red Queen interrupted.

The problem with numbers in French is that to count, you must utilize arithmetic—specifically, addition and multiplication. In the United States and most of the civilized world, children learn the numbers first and then learn to use those numbers in mathematics, but in France you need to know some mathematics in order to learn the numbers. To count, you must multiply; to multiply, you must count; to count, you must multiply . . . It's a numerical Möbius strip.

Things go fairly smoothly until *soixante-neuf.* If you don't speak French and that number rings a bell, congratulations: you've read your *Kama Sutra* (or your *Joy of Sex,* which, to its credit, used the classy French numeral rather than the cruder English "sixty-nine"). *Soixante-neuf* is the last "easy" number in French. Should you want to turn your lovemaking up a notch to seventy, you'll find out there is no "seventy" in French. This is undoubtedly due to French frugality. A country that doesn't have a dedicated word for weather (*temps* can refer to either time or weather) isn't about to waste a word on "seventy." Just add ten to sixty. Thus, after sixty-eight and sixty-nine, there's "sixty-ten" (*soixante-dix*), followed by "sixty-eleven" and so on, right up through sixty-nineteen. But they've already employed this additive strategy in naming their high teens—nineteen is itself ten plus nine (*dix-neuf*)—so seventy-nine is sixty plus ten plus nine: *soixante-dix-neuf.*

Well, you may be wondering, how far are they going to go with this? Is every remaining number up to a hundred going to be based on sixty? Of course not. We haven't done any multiplying yet. The next number, eighty, is *quatre-vingts,* literally "four twenties." Guess what ninety is: *quatre-vingt-dix.* That is, four times twenty, plus ten. You continue in this fashion until you hit ninety-nine, the tongue-twisting, five-syllable, SAT-suitable *quatre-vingt-dix-neuf.*

We say "ninety-nine." They say *quatre-vingt-dix-neuf.* You could get orally injured singing "Ninety-Nine Bottles of Beer on the Wall" in French.

To recap, the French use a base-ten (decimal) numerical system from one through sixty, after which they switch to a base-twenty (vigesimal) system. There are other cultures, including the Mayans and the Basques, who use a vigesimal system, but to my knowledge, French is the only language that uses a mixture of decimal and vigesimal, probably a result of the unification of several number systems in existence in France after the Revolution.

By the way, this base-twenty concept shouldn't be totally foreign to you. Abraham Lincoln harkened back to a vigesimal system when he began the Gettysburg Address, "Four score and seven years ago," but since Americans are lousy at math, it never caught on as a replacement for "eighty-seven."

Think I'm making too big a deal of this oddity? Well, the "four times twenty" stuff was serious enough to split the franco-phone world. In Belgium and Switzerland—even in Rwanda, where half the population tried to exterminate the other half, sometimes even if they were married to them—they had enough common sense to invent words for "seventy," "eighty," and "ninety": *septante, huitante, and nonante.* Just don't say *huitante-trois* in France, or you risk being taken for either a Belgian or an idiot, and it doesn't much matter which: in France they are synonymous. But that's a topic for another day. My problem right now is how do I say I'm fifty-seven when I can't remember the French word for "fifty"? I sputter for what seems like an eternity. Finally I ask, "*Comment dit-on 'fifty' en français?*"

"*Ne parlez pas anglais!*" Mademoiselle D—— scolds me, and I almost feel her tugging me by the ear. Jeez . . . how can I ask this question without using one word of English? My mind races.

Ha! I do remember how to say "forty-nine." "*Quel est le nombre après quarante-neuf?*"

"*Cinquante.*"

"*J'ai cinquante-sept ans.*" Whew! (Okay, so score one for the immersion approach.) We move on to the future tense. I knew the future tense. Two weeks ago. Problem is, now I'm just getting into the past imperfect, which is quite similar, on my podcasts, and I'm confusing the two. How do you conjugate the future? I don't know, because Rosetta Stone hasn't given me the actual rules, only examples that I'm supposed to "absorb." Everything I say is wrong. Nervous, I start stammering in French as if I'm back in Madame D——'s junior high class. What if I just close the program or feign a computer crash? Will I get blacklisted from future classes? Would that be such a bad thing?

Eventually, mercifully, the class ends, and I'm not sure who's more relieved. I change out of my sweat-soaked shirt and drive in to work, thoroughly rattled and feeling fifteen again. That very night I wake before dawn, feeling really strange, as if a sparrow has hatched in my chest during the night and is flapping its wings, trying desperately to get out. I put two fingers to my neck but can't pick up a clear pulse. I wake Anne, who, being a physician, can. It's over two hundred.

"AFib," she says. Next thing I know, I'm being whisked into an emergency room bay. An EKG confirms that my heart is in atrial fibrillation (AFib), a type of arrhythmia where the atria flutter out of rhythm with the rest of the heart owing to a short circuit of sorts in the heart's nervous system. The fluttering itself will not kill me, but if one of the clots that can form in the blood that's sloshing around in the atria moves out and reaches the brain, it's *au revoir.* Thus the first thing they do in the ER is to start an intravenous anticoagulant in my arm. Meanwhile the doctor quizzes me. Any unusual alcohol consumption? No. Drugs? Don't be silly. He continues down the list, and I continue shaking my head. No reason for this to have popped up now—none! Finally he asks, "Any new stress in your life?"

We lock eyes.

"Well, I *am* studying French."

The Event

· ·

"Suppose I wanted to—have a party?" I said.

"Like, what kind of a party?"

"Suppose I wanted Noam Chomsky explained
to me by two girls?"

"Oh, wow . . . You'd have to speak with
Flossie," she said. "It'd cost you."

—WOODY ALLEN, "The Whore of Mensa," 1974

Unable to sleep in my room in the telemetry ward—with two
intravenous lines in my right arm and a blood-pressure cuff and
heart monitor connections on my left, I am virtually chained to
the bed, unable to turn over or get comfortable—I switch on
the TV and come across an infomercial that I have more than
a passing interest in. "Learn a language the way you learned it
as a child," the host says. What does that mean, exactly? How

did I learn language as a child? As I recall, I picked up English pretty easily without conjugation charts or language tapes. And that's the paradox that all linguists grapple with: For infants, language comes effortlessly. It is a skill that virtually every child, regardless of his or her intelligence, masters by the age of three or four. Witness this conversation between a three-year-old and Art Linkletter, from his popular 1950s television show *People Are Funny*. Linkletter has just asked the boy, "And who is in your family, Scott?"

"My mommy, my daddy, and my brother Henry. Oh, and when Daddy goes away on business trips, Uncle John comes and stays with Mommy."

Safe to say that language is acquired before the filters that govern its use are in place. Yet for adults, learning a new language is work, hard work, and we fail far more often than we succeed. How do children manage to do it so easily? It's an unfair contest because babies are born with a head start on language. With really not much else to do, they've been listening to the chatter on the other side of the womb since about the thirtieth week of gestation, and they emerge with a demonstrable familiarity with their mother tongue.

How do we know what's going on in babies' heads? In one experiment, scientists Jacques Mehler and Peter Jusczyk ingeniously fitted a baby's bottle with a nipple that, when sucked on, would play a tape of either spoken French or Russian. The researchers found that four-day-old French babies suck harder when they hear French than when they hear Russian, and that their sucking picks up in intensity when the tape switches from Russian to French, but not when switching from French to Russian.

As an unrepentant Francophile, I'd like to think that this is because French is the most beautiful, most melodic language in the world, but if you do the experiment with Russian babies, they show a preference for Russian over French. Interestingly, the experiment yields the same results even if the audio is muddled so that specific words cannot be distinguished. In other words, after just ninety-six hours out of the womb (and most likely from birth, but there's a limit to how early you can rip a newborn from its mother's breast for a linguistics experiment),* babies have already picked up the cadence, the rhythm, and the characteristic sounds of the language.

And languages do differ greatly in this respect. You can easily tell when someone is using French or Italian even if you don't speak a word of it yourself. Italian draaaws out and almost sings its syllables, as if every sentence is from an operetta, and is filled with *i* and *o* sounds, while French uses hardly any variation in intonation at all and is distinguished by its nasal vowels. Scandinavian languages feature hard *g* sounds that emanate from the nether regions of the throat. In fact, Belgian scientists have determined that newborn babies cry in their mother's tongue,

* Late-breaking news: the limit has just been lowered to seven hours, in a recent experiment by a Swedish team that confirmed the results of the earlier study. I'm sure it's only a matter of time before they figure out a way to do this experiment in vitro.

meaning, for example, that French babies cry with a character-istically French rising inflection.

This ability of babies to distinguish and learn the sounds of their native language comes at a price, though, and one that gets to the root of a problem that vexes many adult foreign language learners: our inability to reproduce some of the pho-nemes (a phoneme is the smallest distinct unit of sound) of that language. We all know the difficulty, for example, that native speakers of Asian languages have with the English letters *r* and *l*—the "flied lice" problem of bad Chinese-waiter jokes.

What is less widely known is that the core problem isn't that they can't pronounce these two letters; they can't pronounce the letters because they can't even aurally *distinguish* between them. To the ear of someone who has grown up surrounded by the Chinese or Japanese languages, which don't employ the *r* and *l* phonemes, *rice* and *lice* actually sound the same.

Infant brains, unlike adult brains, can distinguish all the thousands of different sounds that make up human speech, but that skill is short lived. Researchers have found that seven-month-old Japanese babies can easily discriminate the sound of an English *r* from an English *l*. Yet by the age of ten months, these same babies can no longer tell the difference. This makes me feel a little better about the fact that I cannot master the French *u* sound as in *tu* or the guttural *r* in *rouge* because we don't have anything quite like either in the English language.

You wouldn't know that from watching this Rosetta Stone infomercial, where everyone seems to speak foreign languages perfectly with no effort. I turn it off and eventually fall asleep, which is the signal for the phlebotomist to show up to draw blood again, for only the seventh time today. I don't mind too much, but my poor veins shrivel up and hide whenever Miss Transylvania walks in the door. Well, the veins had better get used to it. I've been told I'm going to be here awhile, at least several days, perhaps as much as a very long week, or until my heart returns to a normal rhythm.

"Courage," the cardiologist says to me, patting me on the shoulder as he leaves the room during morning rounds. It's the first time I've ever heard an American other than Dan Rather use that valediction.* I smile to myself, recalling the French taxi driver who'd good-naturedly wished us "*Courage!*" when we told him we were from the States. *Courage,* one of those words the French use a lot (pronounced "*cour-AHJ*," the accent on the second syllable), and in different ways, is from the French *cœur,* or "heart." Thus *courage* means literally to "have heart," a connection which, sadly, is totally lost in English. However, many of the heart-related idioms we have in our language—"heartbroken," "bighearted," "learn by heart," "lionhearted"—have surprisingly close French equivalents, more so than with most idioms, which tend to be localized. The heart, it seems, is a special case. Mine in particular is real special.

Courage indeed. If I'm going to be imprisoned here for a

* "Courage!" was Rather's much-ridiculed evening news broadcast sign-off for one week in the 1980s.

week, shackled to intravenous drips and monitors, I'd best stop whining and make use of the time. After all, the Marquis de Sade didn't spend twenty years moping about the indignity of confinement (and the lack of young girls and younger boys) while imprisoned in Vincennes; he wrote like mad.* It occurs to me that for at least the next several days I have no job to go to, no appointments, and no obligations whatsoever. I don't have to cook, and—the lazy man's dream—I don't even have to get out of bed to pee. (Which is a good thing, since with multiple IVs dripping into me I have to go about every twenty minutes—all that liquid has to go somewhere.) Why, I can spend all day and half the night studying French!

In theory. This bird fluttering inside my chest is a little distracting. Discussions of the difficulties baby boomers face in learning a language tend to center around our brains, ignoring the other eight-ninths of us that's holding up that head. My heart troubles are not making things any easier, for sure, and I realize, as I lie in my hospital bed, that I've come to a crossroads, *un carrefour*. One path leads to, well, Carrefour, the French department store and supermarket chain; the other, to lots of free time and a free pass—the unassailable excuse that "I gave up French to focus on my health."

Which road will I take? I'm still undecided when Anne asks, "Can I bring you anything from home? A book? Radio?"

---

* I have no idea why I'm comparing myself to the Marquis de Sade. Must be an indication of my state of mind. Or the hospital food.

I think for a moment. "My laptop and headset, the French-English dictionary on my desk, and maybe the collection of Sartre plays in French."

Et puis, merde—screw it! I'm going to Carrefour.

COINCIDENTALLY, ROSETTA STONE, AS if it has been spying on me through the bushes, has moved on to emergency room vocabulary—"hospital," "ambulance," "broken," "burned," "wounded," everything short of *mort*. This is considerate of them, but it means that there are a whole lot of more useful words we'll never get to. Like "draft beer." If I want to order a draft beer in Paris, I'm out of luck if relying on Rosetta Stone; linguistically, I'm better off showing up at a French hospital with a broken collarbone.

The most difficult part of French so far is remembering the new words. This is frustrating, especially considering that the typical child entering kindergarten has a vocabulary of fourteen thousand words. To put that into perspective, a child is learning a new word every two hours of every waking moment. Without trying. How does this almost magical acquisition of language happen? I'm killing myself trying to learn French; who taught me English?

UNTIL THE RENAISSANCE, LANGUAGE was thought to be bestowed on humankind by God, or the gods. The ancient Greeks credited Prometheus with bringing to earth not only

fire but language as well, although as far back as the third century BC, Epicurus (whose writing credits include publishing
the Western world's first cookbook) argued that language is not
the creation of a god, but rather a biological function akin to
vision. Nevertheless, the view of language as something mysti-
cal, inexplicable, or God-given prevailed and may explain the
comparatively late start of the science of linguistics. A book
by the Swiss philosopher and linguist Ferdinand de Saussure,
Course in General Linguistics, published shortly after his death
in 1913, is considered to mark the inception of modern linguistics, putting the science of language a century or two behind
the founding of biology, chemistry, and psychology—even half
a century behind Darwin.

Into the mid-1800s, linguistics research and activity were focused mainly on vocabulary and on cataloging and translating
newfound languages (helped in no small part by Bible societies, which provided the funding for researchers to go into
remote areas, discover and learn an undocumented language,
and translate the Bible into that language). If there was interest
in the origin and nature of language, it was largely relegated
to the realm of psychology—until 1957, that is, when what is
still remembered as "the event" shook up the sleepy world of
linguistics.

The event was the publication of *Syntactic Structures* by
Noam Chomsky, a professor of linguistics at MIT. Chomsky's
book moved the discussion from vocabulary to syntax—that

is, the fundamental rules of language—and raised an interesting question that, surprisingly, hadn't been given a lot of thought until then: How is it that a young child, with limited cognitive development, can acquire such a complex, daunting skill as language? Especially considering that a toddler trying to make sense of the babble around him is surrounded not only by grammatically correct language but also by incorrect, incomplete, and garbled sentences (think of the Watergate tapes). Yet the child somehow learns the syntactic rules of language, that "John hit Mary" is not at all the same as the reversed "Mary hit John," but that "John threw the ball to Mary" *does* mean the same as the reversed "John threw Mary the ball." Language isn't acquired from mere mimicry, Chomsky argued, or children wouldn't say things like, "Tommy hitted me."

Furthermore, language involves combining a finite set of words into an infinite set of combinations and meanings, and Chomsky wondered how children are able to develop a rule system, not only for the finite sentences they've heard, but also for the infinite variations of sentences they haven't heard. Here's an interesting thing about language: Take nearly any sentence on this page, and chances are that this is the first time it's appeared in print. Ever. Yet I was able to effortlessly compose each sentence, almost without thinking. (Let me rephrase that— without thinking about *syntax*.)

This intrigued Chomsky. As did another question: How is it that all the languages of the world, even those that apparently have no common origin, have a common basic grammar, a similar set of rules for how language is constructed? Noam Chomsky's answer to these mysteries of language, the theory that galvanized and divided the world of linguistics in 1957, is that humans are wired for language, are *born* with an innate ability to understand the basic rules of language: what Chomsky calls a universal grammar (UG), a "genetically determined . . . language acquisition device" in the human (and *only* the human) brain.

Chomsky's theory was so divisive that the first question a linguist at a convention in the 1960s was likely to be asked was, "Are you pro-Chomsky or anti-Chomsky?" The detractors claimed that Chomsky was essentially trying to solve a problem that didn't exist; that children learn language from the adults around them; and that the common syntax of the world's languages can be explained by a single, common origin of the world's tongues. Plus, they maintained, the theory falls apart when you look at primitive languages in parts of the world Chomsky didn't probe. There were also objections that the sudden appearance of UG in humans defied the Darwinian theory of natural selection. Yet studies done by, among others, psycholinguists Elissa Newport and Jenny Singleton on deaf children who, even though they weren't exposed to a proper syntax and grammar, "intuitively" used American Sign Language correctly, support Chomsky.

Fifty years after the publication of *Syntactic Structures,* Noam

Chomsky's controversial theories have become nearly universally accepted, as the focus of the research has moved from observational studies to the search for a human "language gene," with some promising but as yet inconclusive results. So accepted is Chomsky's work today that he is as much remembered for his left-of-center politics as for his groundbreaking linguistic theories. Yet his work continues to inspire and spark debate. At my son's wedding reception recently, I found several of his former college classmates sequestered near the bar, engaged in vigorous debate on Chomsky's universal grammar theories as they relate to computer languages. *Plus ça change, plus c'est la même chose.*

As for my own "event," my heart returns to a normal rhythm on the fourth day—I know before the nurses do—and the following morning I go home. The first thing I do is take a long, hot shower, washing my greasy hair three times, scrubbing the smell of hospital off my skin, out of my nostrils. Then I make tea and stare out the window for a long time, watching a soft drizzle, taking comfort in something I used to take for granted: as the French say, *lubb-dupp, lubb-dupp, lubb-dupp.*

Lubb-dupp.

It's Complicated

You can really feel you're having breakfast in Paris
without even making the trip.
—JULIA CHILD on making croissants

*Warning: Do not attempt the activities described in this chapter if
you have any of the following: joint or neck pain, bursitis, arthritis,
a weak back, a weak stomach, a rough week, bad knees, bunions,
an expanding waistline, or anything else to do for the rest of the
day. Or tomorrow.*

Our daughter, Katie, who has two semesters of college French
under her belt (at least she learned from my mistake), is coming
home for her winter break in a few days and is, I fear, expecting
some serious Frenchiness out of her old man when she arrives.
I'd better start cramming for my oral. After breakfast I spend

some time with Fluenz French, which, because it doesn't have a speech recognition engine like Rosetta Stone's, requires you to type in all your responses, thereby putting the focus on written rather than spoken French. I find this laborious and exhausting, not to mention misdirected; I don't expect to be doing a lot of writing in France.

Worse, the on-screen instructor who introduces each lesson in a seven-minute video has a stray lock of hair over one eye that's driving both of us nuts. I'm helpless to do anything about it, but she keeps flipping it back with a little head toss, and I become more occupied with making bets as to when she's next going to toss her head than with listening to what she's saying. It's looking as if Georgetown professor Heidi Byrnes was correct when she warned me about the paucity of self-instruction materials. Or perhaps the problem is just my attention span. Either way, there's not much French going down, so after an hour *I* go down, to the kitchen, in search of a mid-morning snack.

"There's nothing to eat," I say to Anne, sounding, I imagine, like a whining *enfant*.

"What did you want?"

"If we were in France, we'd be munching on croissants right now."

"You want to go to France?"

"I want a croissant."

"Make some."

This from a woman who is intimidated making an omelette

(we'll use the French spelling in this book!). Having planted the seed of a dangerous idea in my head, Anne, as is her fashion, vanishes, her words hanging in the air like the smells wafting from a Parisian *boulangerie*. Make croissants? Interesting concept. Maybe the over-the-top Gallic nature of the activity will stimulate my inspirational French nerve receptors. And even if it doesn't, I'll still have croissants for Katie when she arrives, which with any luck will paper over how bad my French is after what is now six months of daily study.

Having grown up in the 1950s and 1960s, I don't I think I even saw, much less ate, a croissant before going to France. The closest I came was on those special nights when my mom would sharply rap a cardboard cylinder of Pillsbury crescent rolls against the edge of the countertop, unroll and separate the triangular pieces of dough, and wrap them around hot dogs, transforming (or desecrating, depending on your point of view) the most iconic of French foods, the very symbol of the Continental breakfast, into a form of American pop food art that Andy Warhol surely would have approved of. Although I must say that the baked crescent dogs are not half-bad. A little greasy maybe. They're not croissants, or even close to croissants, with or without the hot dog, but they're not bad, and for years my kids wouldn't dream of our having a party without serving bite-size crescent dogs as hors d'oeuvres (a French term meaning "outside the work," originally an architectural term referring to an outbuilding until it was appropriated by chefs for its current use).

The true croissant, although nearly synonymous with France, was actually invented in Austria, where it was called a *Kipferl*— yet another reason to be learning French. Would you rather speak the language that says *Kipferl* or the one that says *croissant,* even if the correct pronunciation of the initial *cr* requires the placement of one's own tongue into a region of the throat that you thought only Linda Lovelace knew about. Legends of the *Kipferl's* origin abound. The most popular one is that it was created in 1683 by Viennese bakers who, up all night baking, heard the invading Ottomans tunneling under the city and gave the alarm. After the victory, they created a roll shaped into a crescent, invoking the Ottoman flag. A colorful tale, but it's probably as true as the story that the baguette was inspired by Napoleon, who insisted his bakers create a loaf that could be strapped to his soldiers' legs.

What is true is that an Austrian baker, August Zang, introduced the *Kipferl* to France when he opened a Viennese bakery in Paris around 1839. An instant sensation, its unique flakiness and butteriness the result of four dozen alternating layers of butter and dough, the roll became known as a *croissant,* the French word for "crescent," which, by the way, explains the appetizing lunar event that happens every month between a new moon and a quarter moon, *un croissant de lune.* (Does "crescent moon" sound as crazily romantic to a Frenchman as *croissant de lune* sounds to an American? Somehow I doubt it, which is yet another reason to . . . you know.)

Although I've never made croissants or any other kind of *viennoiserie* (a yeast dough enriched with eggs, sugar, and milk), I'm an experienced amateur bread baker, so I figure, how hard can it be? I have all the ingredients—flour, butter, milk, egg, and yeast—in the house. And it certainly promises to be a more enjoyable way to spend a morning than figuring out when to use *depuis* and *il y a* to mean "for" and "since," as in "I've been making croissants for seven hours now" and "It seems like forever since I started making these croissants." And that is precisely what I'll be saying in seven hours, in addition to some choice French swear words. But for now, I tune my Internet radio to a station broadcasting out of Aix-en-Provence, get my Julia Child down from the bookshelf, and go to work to the sounds of French *chansons*. The recipe, in case you want to try this at home:

JULIA CHILD'S CROISSANTS

(Adapted by William Alexander for the Twenty-First-Century Home)

1. *La première heure:* Mix flour, salt, yeast, milk, and water into a very tight (that's bakerspeak for dry) dough and work it until your fingers start to cramp up. Place in fridge to chill for two hours.

2. *La troisième heure:* Observe belatedly that Julia notes, "The minimum time required for making croissants is 11 to 12 hours." Figure out how to cut a few corners while working

up a sweat trying to roll out the dough, which has the con-
sistency of Play-Doh and keeps springing back to its original
shape. Take out your frustration on the butter: Julia instructs
you to whack the cold butter repeatedly with a rolling pin,
beating it into submission until it's a rectangle that fits into
the center of the dough (I never knew you could soften butter so quickly that way—good to remember). Note Julia's
warning to work quickly and keep dough and butter chilled
at all times or risk greasy mess. When doorbell rings, fran-
tically wash hands and run to find two Jehovah's Witnesses
who have all morning to discuss the matter of your saving.
Explain it's your croissants that need saving, take the literature, run back to kitchen, fold warming dough into thirds,
and chill for thirty minutes. Roll out dough again, fold, and
chill. Observe that rolling this dough is like trying to skin
an antelope. A live one. Take two ibuprofen to ease pain in
shoulder.

3. *La quatrième heure:* While dough is chilling, watch video
of Julia Child making croissants. Her dough isn't nearly as
tight as mine, although by the end of kneading, she, too, is
audibly out of breath. Note that she is assisted in her task
by a rolling pin the size of a small birch tree. Picking up one
of her smaller pins (that is, one about the size of mine), she
mutters, "I don't know why I ever bought this thing!" and
tosses it into the garbage. I've always loved Julia Child, but at
this moment I love her for a new reason that's just occurred

to me: Julia went to France and . . . became French! I can do this, I tell myself. If she could, I can. Julia is now panting heavily. She would never get on TV today, which tells you about the sad state of TV today.

4. *La sixième heure:* While dough is chilling, watch video of Steve Martin and Meryl Streep making croissants on the spur of the moment in the middle of the night at the bakery owned by Streep's character. Oh, please! The movie is called *It's Complicated,* which certainly does not refer to their making of croissants. They are having a barrel of laughs, but Streep has a sheeter, which does all the rolling, and a good film editor, who cuts out all the chilling. And when it comes to croissants, there isn't much else. Meanwhile, back in my kitchen I'm wrestling with the dough and not laughing at all. After four folds, or "turns," my dough, according to Julia, now has fifty-five layers! Which explains the ache in my lower back. Take two more ibuprofen.

5. *La septième heure:* Into the seventh hour, you may be reminded of the Ingmar Bergman movie *The Seventh Seal,* which is not, I warn you, a tale of a half-dozen semiaquatic marine mammals, but is about a knight who loses a chess match with Death. Lesser known is the sequel, in which Death develops a strange affinity for *viennoiserie.* Finally, after seven hours, having shaved four hours off Julia's most optimistic estimate through judicious use of the freezer, we are ready to bake. As Julia would say, *Bon appétit!*

THE CROISSANTS ARE DELICIOUS, and ready just as Anne comes home. "You made croissants?" she says, sounding surprisingly incredulous. "I was only joking."

You don't say.

"Was it a lot of work?"

"About as easy as learning French."

She takes a bite. "Oh, God, these are good! Let's do this every Sunday!"

A Rooster in the Henhouse

Because it is a female and lays eggs, a chicken is masculine.

—DAVID SEDARIS

Katie and I stand back and admire our work. "What do you suppose Mom's going to think?" Katie asks as we put away the black markers and Post-it notes.

"I don't know, but I can't wait to see her reaction."

"Hey, we forgot one. Do you know the word for this?" Katie asks, pointing to the toaster.

"No idea."

Katie has taken two years of college French but hasn't yet had to make toast, so she looks the word up in the dictionary. "*Grille-pain*. I love it! A bread grill! Can I have a sticky?"

"Masculine or feminine?"

"Masculine."

Katie writes *le grille-pain* on a blue Post-it note and sticks it on the toaster. "*Fini!*" We have labeled everything in sight, from the dishwasher (*le lave-vaisselle*), the sink (*l'évier*), and the garbage (*la poubelle*) to the plastic lobster (*le homard*) on the wall, not to mention the wall (*le mur*), papering the room in a dazzling mosaic of Post-it notes. It's taken some time, because we've had to look up the gender of nearly all these objects. There is no logic to the assignment of gender in French. Partly because Rosetta Stone gives no guidance in this whatsoever, I have been laboring for the longest time under the common misconception that there was a rhyme and reason to gender assignment, that the object itself held the key to its gender, that girly things were feminine and manly things masculine.

Knowing the right gender is important, for gender affects the article that precedes the noun. Who would've thought that of all the words to translate into French, the two that would give me the most difficulty would be "a" and "the." It's hard for us English speakers to even wrap our heads around the facts that (1) inanimate objects have a sex, and (2) the sex changes both the article (*le/la, un/une, mon/ma*) that precedes the object and any adjectives that describe it (*un petit problème/une petite robe*).

Gender even infiltrates a common phrase like "this one," which is *celui-ci* if the thing you're referring to is masculine— say, a woman's breast. If it's a beard, which is obviously feminine (catching on?), it's *celle-ci*. Of course, breasts usually come in pairs, so you'd better know that "those" plural masculine breasts are *ceux-là*, while plural feminine beards are *celles-là*. This French version of "dem and dose" has at least eight variations to be memorized.

Faced with masculine breasts and feminine beards, masculine arms and feminine legs, a cup of hot water that, once you drop a teabag into *her* transgenders into *him,* English speakers look for some kind of logic in gender assignment. This is a mistake. Witness the online language site that posed the pseudo-Freudian rule that objects that are concave (say, a bowl, *bol*) are feminine, while those that are convex, pointed, or aggressive (a fork, *fourchette*) are masculine. This despite the fact that "vagina" is masculine and "necktie," that most phallic piece of men's apparel, is feminine. Well, Katie has just set me straight in the kitchen, where, by the way, we have *le bol* and *la fourchette.*

"It has nothing to do with the nature of the object, Dad. But sometimes you can tell from the ending of the word." A quick check of one of her old textbooks confirms that nouns ending in *-eau* and *-age* are nearly always masculine, while those that end in *-ion* are almost always feminine. There are a few other generalizations as well, but for the vast bulk of the language, you just have to memorize it. On rare occasions you can make an educated guess. Hens are females, roosters male, although chickens are, somewhat counterintuitively, male. For some animals you may have to peek underneath; a male turkey is a *dindon* while a female is a *dinde.* By the time it winds up on white bread with mayo, your guess is as good as mine.

Historian David McCullough relates the story of a mob from the Paris Commune (yet another in a series of French uprisings, this one in 1871) descending on the estate of an American, Charles Moulton, intending to take possession of every animal on the property and quite possibly to slaughter Moulton and his family. Moulton, a slight man with glasses and an atrocious accent, stepped out to face the crowd. As McCullough writes, "No sooner did Moulton open his mouth to reply than the crowd began to giggle, his pronunciation working its spell. When, raising his voice to an unusually high pitch, he declared they could have the horse, '*le cheval*,' but not '*le vache*,' using the masculine pronoun *le* for cow, it was more than they could bear."

Convulsed in laughter, the mob departed with the family horse, but left *le cow*, and more importantly, the family survived.

French is far from alone in having genders. So do Spanish, Hindi, Portuguese, Hebrew, Russian, German, French, Italian, Punjabi, and Urdu. It's English that's the oddball, being the only one of the entire Indo-European family of languages in Europe without gender assignments. (Although, strictly speaking, English does have what is called a biological gender that shows up in words like "actor" and "actress," that is, those words whose genders have worked themselves directly into the nouns.) But all genders are not created equal. In some languages, such as Italian, where nouns that end in *o* are masculine and those that end in *a* are feminine, the genders are a little easier to figure out. After all, that rule covers about half the Italian language right there.

Once you move away from the Indo-European languages, especially to isolated societies, you have a better chance of detecting some method to the gender madness. The misleading Internet post about concave objects being feminine would be fairly accurate if discussing not French but the Manambu language, spoken in Papua New Guinea, where small and rounded things are feminine, and big and long ones are masculine. Or the Australian aboriginal language of Tiwi, where a blade of grass is masculine, but a patch of grass is feminine. I swear, a Freudian could have a field (*feminine*) day delving into this stuff.

And genders are not restricted to, well, gender. A number of languages add a vegetable gender—his, hers, and eggplant—used to refer to plants and to things derived from plants, like wood. Given that gender is determined by the nature of the object in these long-unchanged languages, it is likely that the Indo-European family of languages also had a more transparent gender system at one point, but that it got corrupted, possibly when it lost the third gender that all the descendants of Latin, including French, Italian, and Spanish, had at one time: the neuter. This was a handy gender that was used for inanimate objects without a clear phallic or feminine association, and as it fell into disuse, tables and chairs had to take on either masculine or feminine genders, which is when things got messy.

The neuter survives in German today, resulting in, as linguist John McWhorter puts it, "such user-hostile cases as each piece of silverware in German having a different gender: spoons are boys, forks are girls, knives are hermaphrodites." And girls are neuter. Go figure: *Fräulein* (unmarried woman), *Mädchen* (girl), and *Weib* (wife or woman) are all neuter. This caught Mark Twain's attention.

In German, a young lady has no sex, while a turnip has. Think what overwrought reverence that shows for the turnip, and what callous disrespect for the girl. See how it looks in print—I translate this from a conversation in one of the best of the German Sunday-school books:

GRETCHEN: Where is the turnip?

WILHELM: She has gone to the kitchen.

GRETCHEN: Where is the accomplished and beautiful English maiden?

WILHELM: It has gone to the opera.

Since English is originally derived from German, it must have had genders at one time, so we have a mystery on our hands. How, and why, did genders disappear from English?

Old English had all three German genders, and it wasn't until the eleventh century, during the early Middle English period, that their use began to decline, as the neuter gender—our modern "the"—began to be used for all nouns. Did the 1066 invasion of England by a foreign force with their la-di-da *les* and *la*s and *un*s and *une*s hasten the decline? The evidence is sketchy on this, but it has been speculated that when French became the language of the educated class in England, English became stamped as the language of the *un*educated class, and the educators—those who make or enforce the rules of languages—lost interest in it, leaving the peasants free to do as they wished.

What they wished was to make language simpler. So, while the English-cum-French speakers of the court were trying to figure out why the French word *personne* was always feminine, regardless of the sex of the person you were referring to, the peasants just took the French word, absorbed it into English as a neutered noun, and went out to milk the neutered cow. Life was too short and too hard for a peasant to worry about how to address the bloody cow.

Gender, of course, is still going strong in France. And that raises an interesting question: Because a Frenchman must refer to a fork as "her" and "she," and must think, *C'est ma fourchette,* when musing about his fork, does he think of it, subconsciously or otherwise, as a feminine object with womanly properties? When he thinks of his beloved cheese, *son fromage,* is there anything homoerotic going on, or is his use of the pronoun just habit—a second-nature kind of thing that means nothing, a verbal one-night stand? Fortunately, linguists have attempted to answer this question, and the answer may surprise you.

Maria Sera, a psychologist at the Institute of Linguistics at the University of Minnesota, devised an experiment to find out if French and Spanish speakers thought of feminine-gendered objects as actually having feminine traits (and the same for masculine objects). French and Spanish have different gender assignments for some common objects (forks, bananas, cars, beds, clouds, screws, and butterflies, to name a few), so Sera recruited native French and Spanish speakers who were told they were assisting in the preparation of a movie in which inanimate objects come to life. The volunteers were shown a series of pictures, without labels, and asked to choose between a man's and a woman's voice for each object. When French adult speakers saw their feminine fork, *la fourchette,* the vast majority of them (twenty-six out of thirty-two) wanted a female voice; when Spanish speakers saw their masculine fork, *el tenedor,* the majority of them (nineteen out of thirty-two) wanted a masculine voice.

Consider the screw. It would have to be a penis to appear any more masculine, and in Spanish it is in fact a masculine noun. When shown a picture of a screw, only two of thirty-two Spanish speakers gave it a female voice. The French, however, have assigned the screw a feminine gender, and after viewing the same picture, eleven—nearly a third—of the French speakers gave it a feminine voice. The experiment, unfortunately, did not include any biological objects with clearly counterintuitive genders (beards, chickens, or vaginas), but it did include a peanut, the word for which is feminine in French, and to which the majority of French speakers assigned a masculine voice. I'm no scientist, but I'll humbly suggest that the results were skewed by what researchers call interference—in the guise of that international celebrity Mr. Peanut.

In another study involving German and Spanish, native speakers were asked to ascribe characteristics—strong or weak, big or little—to objects that diverged in those two languages. Here again, the gender of the objects influenced the answers. Bridges and clocks, which are masculine in Spanish, were judged to be stronger by Spaniards than by Germans, who in turn favored their masculine chairs and keys.

It has been suggested that English has lost something by dropping gender, that languages are a little richer, a bit more romantic, when they wax poetically on *la lune* or *la mer,* that giving sexual properties to objects enriches the language and the spirit. Perhaps it does. I'll ponder that the next time I have a fork in my mouth.

ONE BENEFIT OF THIS gender game is that it's provided some color for our repapered kitchen wall, since I've used blue Post-it notes for the masculine objects and pink for the feminine, a touch I'm particularly proud of. Katie and I stand back to admire our work. "*Pas mal,*" I say. Not bad at all, she responds in French, and I respond back. Actually, there is a term for this: conversation. Katie's French is far better than mine, but I'm able to sustain a primitive conversation with her, albeit one strewn with so many errors in both directions that we may be speaking something closer to a patois than to real French. Nevertheless the satisfaction of this brief conversation gives me an idea. I suggest—in French, of course—that we continue speaking to each other in French.

"*Toute la journée?*" she asks. All day?

"*Non, non, ma petite. Tous les jours.*" Every day.

She looks as alarmed as if I'd just told her she has to make crêpes Suzette for the French ambassador in thirty minutes. But Katie loves a challenge, and we shake on the deal, although with one caveat. She is a little concerned about my study habits and, it must be said, not unhappy to be able to turn the tables after twelve years of enduring my nagging her about homework. As I'd feared, she is aghast that after half a year of intensive study, I haven't learned to conjugate even regular verbs. That's basic to learning the language, she insists, no matter what Rosetta Stone says.

"*Il n'y a pas de . . . de* shortcuts," she says. She leaves the kitchen and returns with an inch-tall stack of her old five-by-seven-inch index cards from high school, one each for all the regular verbs that end in *-er, -re,* and *-ir,* plus one for each irregular verb. I run down the first card: *je fais, tu fais, il fait, nous faisons, vous faites, ils font . . .* Now the future tense: *je ferai, tu feras, il fera . . .*

"*C'est plus difficile que Rosetta Stone,*" I say, not looking forward to this at all.

"*Juste dix minutes chaque jour!*" Katie implores, adding that she usually did her ten minutes at bedtime.

"*D'accord*," I say, sighing. There's just one little problem with our little immersion camp, I point out.

"*Ooh! Maman!*"

Anne is going to feel quite left out, if not downright lonely, when Katie and I speak only French for the next month, until Katie returns to school. I haven't yet figured out how to deal with the situation when Anne comes home from work, but I run to the kitchen to capture her reaction to our decorating job, throwing on every light in the room. This should be priceless. Dropping her bag on the kitchen table, she takes off her coat and asks, "What did you do today?"

Look up, woman! "Um, a little French."

Hanging her keys on the hook above the steam radiator, she sees the word *radiateur* in Katie's handwriting. "Oh, is Katie helping you?" Anne then starts to head out of the kitchen, oblivious to the other two dozen notes peppering her kitchen.

"Notice anything?" I practically shout.

Anne surveys the room. Anne surveys me. Just then, Katie comes in.

"*Bonsoir, Papa!*"

"*Bonsoir, Katie! Ça va?*"

"*Bien. Et toi?*"

Anne looks from me to Katie and back to me. "*Maman*,"

Katie says, explaining (in French) that she and I are speaking only French for the rest of her winter break. Katie asks if Anne wants to join us.

"*¡Sí—por supuesto!*" Anne chirps enthusiastically.

Hoo boy. Going to be an interesting month.

Die Hard

. . . .

> They are about to be taught a lesson in the real
> use of power. You will be witnesses.
> —*Die Hard,* 1988

I study French late into the night, reading a story from a dual-language book of short stories, the original French on the left pages and the English translation opposite. This sounds as if it would be an easy way to learn the language, but I often have difficulty matching the corresponding English to the French. When in the controlled environment of Rosetta Stone and Fluenz, I feel encouraged by my progress; yet one step into the real francophone world, even in print, and the task feels overwhelming.

The book still on my lap, I fade into a restless, jumpy sleep, dreaming again of French—even, I think, dreaming a little *in*

French. Then, as dreams are wont to do, the scene seamlessly but inexplicably shifts to a hospital, where no less than six white-gowned doctors and nurses are bent over me as I struggle to hold consciousness. Fragments of conversation drift over me, just beyond my grasp. "Eighty over sixty." "I can't get a vein." "Sixty over forty." "I need that IV *now!*" "I have to ask you to leave the room." "I love you."

No, don't leave the room! Get them a vein; you know my veins! But Anne does leave, and eventually the others, too, and I'm left with a foreign-accented doctor with more than a passing resemblance to the spooky-looking actor Peter Lorre. He asks me a question, but something is amiss: his accent isn't French. This dream isn't going right. *Why isn't this dream going right?*

The doctor repeats his question, slowly, looking me in the eye. "Do you have any jewelry or false teeth?" he asks again. What a question! Is he buying or selling?

"No," I mumble. Interview over. He injects something into my vein. The room goes soft, then black.

"Clear!"

Oh, *merde!* Three hundred joules of electricity shoot into my chest, entering my body through the electrode patch positioned on my chest and passing straight through my heart, exiting via the patch directly opposite on my upper back. They haven't given me enough anesthesia, and the shock jolts me awake. My body twitches violently, nearly levitating, I'm later told by a nurse—you may think you've seen this on TV a million times, but trust me, you really haven't—then settles back down onto the gurney, and I feel my lids closing again. This is the kind of half dream you want to wake up from, and fast. Fortunately, I get help.

"Wake up, Mr. Alexander, wake up," I hear a voice exhorting me. Of course, this is no dream. I have just been defibrillated. *Lubb-dupp. Lubb-dupp.* Two months after my previous episode, my heart has lapsed not into AFib but into another form of arrhythmia called tachycardia, which, in the cool, cockpit-style prose of my doctor, my body "is not tolerating well." The electric charge used to jump-start my quivering atria is enough to turn over a car engine, a surprisingly apt analogy, because when I look over my shoulder to see the defibrillation unit, I spot the unmistakable outlines of an automotive battery hidden inside a plastic casing.

"That's what they use?" I say to Anne when she is allowed to return. "I've been defibrillated with . . . a DieHard?" (Note to Sears: I am available for product endorsements. Contact my agent.)

Three hundred joules—the kinetic energy of a tennis ball traveling at 4,200 miles an hour—is not only enough to start your car engine, it's also enough to give you what feels like the worst sunburn you've ever had. Late that night, the skin on my chest on fire, I go into the bathroom to put on some salve. In the mirror I see the outline of the large electrode pad, clear as can be, on my chest. It's looks and feels as if I've been branded with a clothes iron. Hours of hydrocortisone, Tylenol, and Silvadene ointment, an ice pack, and two sleeping pills later, I am finally able to fall asleep. In the middle of the night, I wake up retching violently. None of the doctors knows why.

I do. It's my body's way of doing an oil change.

I'M NOT CRAZY ABOUT the idea of traveling while my heart is behaving like a twenty-year-old Citroën—you never quite know what's going to happen when you turn the key in the morning—but six months earlier I'd agreed to a speaking engagement in Maine, and a deal is a deal, and a full month has passed since I thought *I* had passed, so after getting a reserved clearance from my doctor ("Can you get back within a day?"), with beta blockers, antiarrhythmics, and the blood thinner Coumadin in hand, Anne and I head up to Maine, one of our favorite places this side of the Atlantic.

I often get the jitters before speaking, and as I prepare to address this gathering of a hundred or so bread enthusiasts, I recognize that familiar tight feeling in my gut. Well, not exactly the gut. A little higher . . . to the left . . . that's the spot. AFib is often confused with or feels like palpitations, which themselves are often associated with anxiety, so even though there is no hard clinical evidence that anxiety is connected with AFib, whenever I feel anything the least bit unusual in my chest—a little tightening of the gut, a skipped beat, a taco—my left hand flies up to my neck, where I've gotten very good at locating my pulse at the carotid artery, and I need only two beats to confirm that I'm in rhythm.

I've been doing this probably a couple of dozen times a day since my last impersonation of Frankenstein receiving the high-voltage gift of life ("It lives!!!"), and when I do it in public or even (rather, especially) in Anne's presence, I've developed a technique designed to make it seem as if I'm just casually tending to an itch on my neck. I know this compulsive pulse taking is counterproductive behavior, but I can't seem to help it, so fearful am I of returning to arrhythmia, to the hospital, to the DieHard. The anticipation of recurrence is almost worse than the AFib. Thus I've taken the doctor's advice to stay off alcohol. No *vin*, no *bière*, no Grand Marnier. How very un-French! And un-fun.

The talk goes well, and my heart, thank God, is none the worse for it. Afterward, Anne and I drive down to Monmouth, a small town whose landmark is Cumston Hall, a wildly eccentric Romanesque / Queen Anne–style building that has been restored for use as a theater. We go there whenever we're in the area, no matter what's playing, because the repertory company is good and the theater is amazing, the ceiling adorned with cherubs and intricate plaster carvings, and it is *the* place to be for anyone who's part of, or aspires to be part of (oxymoron alert), central Maine society.

Tonight's performance happens to be *Tartuffe; or, The Imposter*, the French farce by Molière, the seventeenth-century

French comic dramatist who is to France what Shakespeare is to England, only funnier. Molière was a fierce satirist of French social manners, customs, hypocrisy, and society in general, as well as of the idiosyncrasies of the still-nascent French language, which especially endears him to me. The plot of *Tartuffe* centers around a holier-than-thou religious charlatan who uses his pious position within a family to seduce both the husband's wife and his daughter right under the husband's nose. The play had a run of exactly one performance, at Versailles in 1664, closing after the archbishop of Paris turned in, shall we say, a bad review to King Louis XIV. As the archbishop happened to be Louis's confessor, the king might have felt a little extra pressure to accede to his wishes.

Religious hypocrisy and seduction of the worst kind being alive and well some 350 years later, *Tartuffe* is still topical, fresh, and quite funny, though the distraction isn't enough to keep me from occasionally surreptitiously monitoring the beating of my heart. I mentioned earlier that I've always felt an affinity to Molière, but the comparison suddenly seems more apt than I'd intended, for in between acts and pulse checks, I learn from the program that Molière spent much of his life in poor health and in the company of doctors, who were unsuccessful in treating his chronic illnesses, which is unsurprising, given that the favored treatments of the day were bloodletting and leeches. As we writers like to say, rotten luck but good material; Molière's experiences with doctors provided him with enough fodder for several new comedies.

Molière's final play, *The Imaginary Invalid,* was inspired by his experiences with the medical profession. Here Argan, a healthy hypochondriac, submits to all kind of outrageous treatments from the doctors treating his nonexistent illnesses. One line in particular rings true for me: "Nearly all men die of their remedies, and not of their illnesses." Molière, despite his illness, was the original "hardest-working man in show business," writing, directing, and acting in his own plays while also managing his theater company. He simply refused to allow his poor health to alter his life or slow him down, and learning that, I'm glad I've come to Maine, despite my reservations. It's been good to get away, hopefully to provide some enjoyment to some people, and to receive a good deal more in return, both from the people I've met at the bread conference and from the actors on the stage.

Molière played the title role in *The Imaginary Invalid* and during just its fourth performance began to cough up blood. Surely some in the audience must have thought it was part of the act. A trouper in the truest sense of the word, he finished the show and died a few hours later, on February 17, 1673.

He was fifty-one years old.

I think about Molière, about his struggles, about the beauty of France, about life. And I leave Maine more determined than ever to learn French.

Ministry of Silly Talks

. . . .

VINCENT: You know what they call a Quarter Pounder with
Cheese in Paris?

JULES: They don't call it a Quarter Pounder with Cheese?

VINCENT: Nah, man, they got the metric system, they
wouldn't know what the fuck a Quarter Pounder is.

JULES: What do they call it?

VINCENT: They call it a Royale with Cheese. . . .

JULES: What do they call a Big Mac?

VINCENT: A Big Mac's a Big Mac, but they call it "*Le* Big Mac."
—*Pulp Fiction*, 1994

The French actually have a national body just for this type
of Big Mac problem, the Académie française, whose job it is
to keep the language pure, and that includes coming up with
French terms for words that wash up on the beaches like so
many foreign invaders. Exactly what, you might ask, is the

Académie française, and who gave them the right to decide what is and what isn't French? Even the name is confusing, for the word *française* (or its masculine equivalent *français*), while simply translated as "French," can refer to the French language, the French people, or a pan sauce of butter and lemon.

There are only two occasions when the academy makes news: the first is when they fulfill their primary duty and complete a new dictionary, which means they haven't needed a press conference since Hitler invaded Poland; the second is when they issue their list of "disapproved" words—the latest, just released, runs some sixty-five pages—on which occasions they are generally derided and sneered at. But the members of the academy seem not to care; they are out of public view 364 days of the year.

But, my, do they make up for it on the 365th day, usually a day in December, when France harkens back to its glory days of empire, recalling the majesty of the Sun King and the power of Napoleon, the day the forty Immortels of the academy march past admiring crowds on their way into the Institut de France for their annual meeting. Emerging incongruously from taxis while attired in green velvet robes and Napoleonic bicornes, swords at their sides, they look as if they're itching for a rematch with Admiral Nelson (which may explain why Jacques Cousteau was once a member).

The phrase "venerable institution" almost seems inadequate for a group that has been meeting nearly without interruption since 1635. That was around the time, remember, that modern French was first gaining ground, the various *langues d'oïl* of the north merging into something that was now being called French. It was also around the time of a new, fashionable social institution: the Parisian salon. And in some of these salons, groups of amateur wordsmiths, poets, and social climbers started meeting regularly to discuss their relatively new language, sort of a book club without the book.

One of these soirées caught the attention of Cardinal Richelieu, the chief adviser to King Louis XIII and the first French theologian to have written in French. Richelieu elevated the group to an official French organization (thus bringing it under government control), calling it l'Académie française. Its mission was to define standards of French vocabulary and grammar—to, as the charter states bluntly, "clean the language of all the filth it has caught" and make French "pure [and] eloquent." And the means by which the Académie would define "pure" French would be to publish an official dictionary. Since written French was still relatively new, and the language sat at the confluence of several linguistic streams, the resulting pool held many of the same fish, but with different names and/or spellings. There was even disagreement on how to pronounce and spell the word for that most French of French foods: cheese.

Printers had already partly taken matters into their own hands by adding diacritics—those little accents of various shapes and sizes, as found in *café* and *Provençal*—to distinguish between similar words and to aid in pronunciation. My favorite diacritic is the *tréma* (as in ö) because it is a diacritic spelled with another diacritic and because the Germans later borrowed it and called it an umlaut, which the *New Yorker* stubbornly continues to use in the word "coöperate," apparently to ensure that the nation's most sophisticated readers don't mistakenly pronounce it "couperate."

The founding members, or Immortels (so called because they are appointed for life), of l'Académie française got right to work and set out to produce the very first dictionary of the French language. A mere fifty-five years later, the dictionary was officially presented, not to King Louis XIII, who was by then dead and buried, but to his son and successor, King Louis XIV, who received it with the dry understatement, "Gentlemen, this is a long-awaited work." And because the Immortels are not actually immortal, the project outlived not only Louis XIII and Richelieu but a fair number of the original forty members as well—the first principal author inconveniently died at the letter *l*. And whenever one of them passed away, a new one was inducted, and they had to debate whether to spell "cheese" *fromage* or *formage* all over again.

Design by committee was a problem independent scholars didn't have, so that by the time the academy's official dictionary finally appeared in print in 1694, several others were already in widespread use, including one produced on the sly by a member of the academy (and they wondered why he was taking such copious notes during their meetings). The academy's dictionary was a critical flop, disparaged for its glaring omissions and circular and outdated definitions. Yet it could've been worse. As the book was going to press, an alert Académie française member realized just in time that they'd left out the word . . . *académie*. Omissions continued to plague subsequent editions. The most recent edition—that is, the one released in 1935—left out *allemand* (German). Do you believe in karma?

Another of the academy's responsibilities is to standardize French grammar. The publication of their first grammar book took exactly 296 years. Which, come to think of it, brings us nearly to the present. The academy, whose recent members have included novelist and filmmaker Marcel Pagnol, former French president Valéry Giscard d'Estaing, and anthropologist Claude Lévi-Strauss, is now working hard on the ninth edition (presumably they'll not leave out the Germans this time). As of this writing, they're up to the letter *p*.

The academy relies on specialized terminology commissions of the French Ministry of Culture for keeping French both current and pure, which more often than not means finding French replacements for new words of foreign influence (nearly all "franglais," a merger of French and English). In theory, the task is straightforward: take a foreign word such as "podcast" and come up with a French equivalent other than *le podcast*. Unfortunately, the tendency of the French to be verbose works greatly to their disadvantage, especially in the Twitter age. The recommended replacement for the seven-letter word "podcast" was *diffusion pour baladeur* ("broadcasting over a Walkman"). For "wi-fi" (which the French pronounce "wee-fee") they came up with *accès sans fil à l'Internet,* literally "access without wire to the Internet." Put them together, and a simple "wi-fi podcast" becomes *diffusion pour baladeur d'accès sans fil à l'Internet.* Sorry, but I don't think the kids are going to go for it. And in the end, when it comes to language, the kids set the rules.

I wonder whether the academy realized that "wi-fi" doesn't even make sense in English. The term exists only because someone in a manufacturer's marketing department, having been given the assignment to come up with a word or phrase *short enough for a sticker on a computer* to describe a wireless network connection, was old enough to remember playing his Charlie Parker albums on his spiffy "hi-fi."

Recently, a reporter from the *Wall Street Journal* was able to sit in on an unintentionally hilarious session of France's General Commission for Terminology and Neologisms, whose members, working at a pace slower than the slowest Godard movie you never saw, were discussing what to do with the new term "cloud computing." Now you'd think this would be an easy one: just call it *informatique en nuage,* which literally means, well, "cloud computing." But no, this seventeen-member group of professors, linguists, scientists, and a former ambassador spent the entire day agonizing over this.

"What? This means nothing to me. I put a cloud of milk in my tea!" one member objected.

"A term that includes 'cloud' causes laughter or at least a smile," protested another.

There was also much hand-wringing over how the expression "in the clouds" means one isn't paying attention or thinking clearly—exactly as in English, although I doubt that a single American has made that connection with "cloud computing"—so the alternative *capacité informatique en ligne* (online computing capacity) was offered up. This had the advantage of affording the acronym CIEL, which, beautifully, is the French word for "sky"!

Parfait, non?

"Going from 'cloud' to 'sky' seems a bit far-fetched," a member complained. *¡Ay, caramba!*

Finally, as the setting sun was reflecting off the Louvre across the street, with no viable alternatives and, I imagine, each of the committee members ready to kill all the others, they adjourned without a solution. Only several months later (with the speed at which technology moves, they're lucky that cloud computing hadn't by then become obsolete) did they agree to fall back to the original and obvious choice: *informatique en nuage*.

While the French regularly ignore the rulings of the academy (you see signs for "wee-fee" everywhere in France), they do respect it and its mission. The French are far more concerned than Americans, not only with the purity of their language, but with its correct usage and pronunciation. They even have a word for a language error—*faute*—which doesn't mean just "fault" or "mistake" but carries a moral or judgmental stigma, unlike a mere *erreur*.

It's hard not to feel a little sympathy for the French, whose language, once *the* international language, the language of diplomacy, business, and culture, has become almost irrelevant. As the magazine *Le Point* put it, "Our technical contribution stopped with the word chauffeur." French attempts to stem the tide of English do have that finger-in-the-dike feel. When the French started *le jogging* and eating *les cheeseburgers* on *le weekend,* the alarmed government, realizing that the academy wasn't doing all that *super* a job in keeping out "the filth," founded, in 1970, the Commission for Terminology.

With no enforcement power, the commission was widely ignored, so just five years later the government passed the Maintenance of the Purity of the French Language act, introducing fines for the use of banned anglicisms (TWA received one for issuing its boarding passes in English), which was followed in 1984 by the General Commission for the French Language, which in turn was succeeded by the 1994 Toubon Law, mandating the use of the French language in all official government publications, commercial contracts, and advertisements, and in all workplaces and public schools.

Yet for all the hullabaloo it is estimated that anglicisms account for only about 1 to 2 percent of all French. Undoubtedly, though, English is encroaching. Will France succeed in keeping France French? Or for that matter, keeping *French* French? It's one thing to legislate, but another thing to get people to give up "wee-fee" for *accès sans fil à l'Internet*. The world has changed greatly since France ruled during the Enlightenment, but one thing hasn't changed: language follows economic power. Thus I may love French, but when I have grandchildren, and they're ready to study a foreign language, I'm going to advise them to learn Mandarin Chinese.

Le Social Network

· ·

We lived on farms, then we lived in cities,
and now we're going to live on the Internet.
—*The Social Network,* 2010

FIFTY-SEVEN-YEAR-OLD WRITER LIVING NEAR NEW YORK
CITY SEEKS PARTNER FOR FRENCH CONVERSATION.
My heart has been shocked again—Anne confirmed that it
took two jolts to restore my rhythm this time (I had suspected
as much because they must've shifted the electrode pad slightly
after the first, unsuccessful shock, leaving a second, slightly off-
set brand on my chest, making me look like a steer on the Double-O Ranch), and then a few weeks later the fluttering bird of
AFib has nested in my chest once again. For good, apparently,
say my doctors, who try to reassure me that my future arrhyth-
mic life will be just fine, once I get used to it, although I'll be
on Coumadin and beta blockers the rest of my days.

Perhaps, but I'm a long ways from being used to it, so I've made an appointment with a cardiac electrophysiology specialist in the city to discuss treatment options. In the meantime, I've posted my profile on MyLanguageExchange.com, having just read that Rosetta Stone, Fluenz, and all the others are obsolete, headed the way of the dinosaur. The asteroid said to be wiping them out is social media, specifically, language-networking sites like the one I've just signed up for. These all work roughly the same way. For a nominal fee or even nothing, you search for a language partner who speaks the language you want to learn and who wants to learn your language. Then you can converse on Skype, either using exercises provided by the website or just chatting freestyle. Some sites take a crowd-sourcing approach, where everyone can see and correct your work. In either case, no intimidating classrooms, no sadistic teachers, no huge costs. Just mano a mano language sharing: you scratch my tongue, I'll scratch yours.

In theory, this sounds great to me. It must to Rosetta Stone as well. They've responded by cutting their price by half and buying out Livemocha, the largest (and most expensive to consumers) of these sites. I save the MyLanguageExchange profile and head to work. Over the weekend, I'll do some outreach and see if I can find a compatible partner.

No need. The very next morning I receive *un bonjour*—the site's mechanism for letting you know when another member wants to contact you—from a French woman named Sylvie.

She's interested in beginning with e-mail correspondence, not Skype, which suits me fine. Sylvie writes, "I can teach you french to help you a lot to improve your level and i'd like you help me to do the same, because i'm on the intermediate level and i'd like speaking currently english." Looks like we are *definitively* on the same level. I follow the link to her profile. Let's see . . . lives an hour south of Paris, is a mostly unemployed twenty-five-year-old model and heavy-metal rock musician.

A perfect match.

I write back, in French, which takes forever—nearly two hours for a short note—because I look up and double-check everything, using Google Translate, a website called Word Reference.com, and a good, old-fashioned dictionary. I tell Sylvie a little about myself, asking that she correct my French, and offering to correct her English. The next day she responds affirmatively, and just like that, I have a French pen pal! I can't wait to tell Anne.

"That's great," she says. "Tell me about him."

HAVING JUST COMPLETED MY first true writing exercise in French—an e-mail to Sylvie—let me say that, while I hate to be diacritical, typing all these damn accents is a royal pain. Sylvie's French keyboard has all the accented letters (often in places where you expect to find other characters, which can drive you *fou* if you've ever tried to write in English on a French computer), but for me to add diacritics requires a laborious

"Insert . . . Symbol" followed by a hunt for, say, the *é*. Yes, I know, I can write macros and reassign keys, but spare me: I can't be expected to learn French and how to use a computer at the same time (and I'm a computer guy!). Especially not with the speed with which Sylvie is replying. I've barely sent off my note when an e-mail pops up, and *Leçon 1* is under way.

> The first mistake is about conjugation for this sentence: "je propose que nous commencer. . . ." this sentence needs to conjugate the verb "commencer" because with the personal pronoun "nous" the sentence is like this: "je propose que nous commençions" (conditional). In a second point, we don't use "très plus difficile" in the same time, it's better to tell "beaucoup plus difficile" :) but it's not an important mistake.

Sylvie's corrections may bruise my ego, but they also lend credence to the social-networking language model. Sylvie is a good teacher. Her corrections far exceed the length of my original notes, for I have errors in every sentence. My genders aren't even correct because I didn't think to look up the nouns that I "knew." Yet Sylvie seems not to mind correcting my French and to have plenty of free time to do it. Having graduated from college as a business major several years ago, she's still looking for her first full-time, permanent job. Youth unemployment is a chronic problem in France, as I've learned from watching TV-5Monde (some programs are subtitled in English), and French businesses have taken advantage of the situation by using "interns"—who often graduated years ago—in ways that would make even American corporations blush. It seems that corporate power is very much alive in the idealistic, socialist state.

French speakers from other states have been contacting me as well. Francophones from Morocco, Algeria, Senegal, and other former French possessions are eager to partner up, but I'm being choosy and only entertaining *bonjours* from France. Besides, at the rate that Sylvie is writing her long, chatty notes, I'm not sure I can handle any more partners, especially since I've found yet another social media resource.

WE GO AROUND THE table, briefly introducing ourselves in French, first names only, making this feel more like an Alcoholics Anonymous meeting than a French Language and Culture Meetup.com gathering. When my turn comes, I feel as if I should say, "*Je m'appelle Bill et je suis un francophile.*"

I was a little wary about attending, because "Meetup.com" sounds like a singles website, and the fact that previous meetings of this French Language and Culture group included a special Valentine's Day event did nothing to dispel that impression.

Well, if Meetup.com is really Pickup.com, this group had better hurry. Some of the members look like they may be touch and go to make it to the next meeting. A woman who has to be at least eighty sits opposite me, and a gentleman not much younger sits next to her. There are twelve of us in all, including the group leader, Gabrielle, a native of Belgium. (My assumption is that a "Belgian Language and Culture" group wouldn't hold the same allure.)

Directed by Gabrielle, we start conversing in primitive, halting French—all but one of us, a poor fellow who has been dragged here by his wife and doesn't speak any French at all. He compensates by making bad jokes, getting up and taking pictures, and generally playing the class clown.

By acting out situations, we expand our vocabularies and have our French corrected by Gabrielle. She has a wonderful sense of humor and seems to be genuinely enjoying hanging out with a bunch of people who are mauling her native tongue. Away from the canned exercises of computer software, I find myself stymied by the amount of preparation and premeditation required to say even the simple sentence, "I'd like to take a taxi to that nice restaurant in the small village." Having to solve a Rubik's Cube of conjugation, gender, and word order before you open your mouth presents quite a barrier to fluid conversation.

It reminds me of when I was teaching Katie to drive a stick shift. Just before shifting, you could see her lips moving, the wheels in her brain spinning as she thought through the steps: Ease back on the gas with the right foot; depress the clutch with the left foot; push the gear lever down, toward the center, and forward; gently release the clutch with the left foot while increasing the gas with the right . . . Darn, it stalled! Now, years later, she does all those things subconsciously. She "speaks stick shift."

My French engine stalls a number of times, but toward the end of the two hours I am able to express the fact that I bake bread at home, and from the other end of the table I hear, "*Pain au levain?*"

"You speak French!?" someone says to the class clown, incredulous.

"Not a word," he says. "But *bread* I know."

The last exercise of the evening is counting backward from twenty. We go around the table, taking turns. When my second turn comes up, all I have to do is say the simple, idiot-proof number "one," *un.*

"Auh," I say with a bit of nasal inflection.

"Auh," Gabrielle corrects me.

"Auh," I say.

"Auh!" she corrects, a little louder, apparently thinking I must be hard of hearing if I can't repeat the simple one-syllable sound she is making, the shortest word in the French language. A Frenchman, a friend of Gabrielle's who's sitting in on the class, chimes in, trying to help me out. I try to imitate the sound, but to my ear I'm saying exactly what they're both saying. How can I correct something that already sounds correct to me?

The problem, of course, is my adult brain, which cannot distinguish between the sounds the native French speakers are making and the ones I am producing. This is compounded in older adults by another problem: We don't hear as well as we used to. Even if we're not hard of hearing, we don't distinguish different sounds and frequencies nearly as well as when we were younger. Gabrielle perseveres, demonstrating the shape my mouth must form to say the nonnasal *un*. I finally get something close enough to satisfy her, but—once again—French is humbling, and my inability to say this simplest of words leaves me feeling a bit foolish as we adjourn for the night.

It goes without saying, I leave without a date.

Making Fanny

> I have sampled every language; French is my favorite.
> Fantastic language, especially to curse with.
> —The Merovingian, in *The Matrix Reloaded*, 2003

Because getting an appointment with Dr. Larry Chinitz, the director of Clinical Cardiac Electrophysiology (and, according to his directory entry, a fluent speaker of Yiddish!) at New York University Langone Medical Center, is more difficult than getting an audience with the pope, I've come into the city early in case I get a flat on the way to the station, the train is late, or the transit workers, inspired by their French counterparts, stage a one-day strike.

None of this happens, which is almost annoying because I hate being early, but I know exactly where to go to fill the time—a Parisian park that sits between Grand Central Terminal and Times Square. No fooling. Bryant Park, which has been described by the city Landmarks Preservation Commission as "a prime example of a park designed in the French Classical tradition," features the green folding chairs and little round metal tables you see in French parks; Le Carrousel, where horses circle endlessly to French music; and, best of all, a *boulodrome.*

A *boulodrome* is where one plays *boules,* although the French generally call their variant *pétanque,* maybe because *boules,* despite being a French word, doesn't have an accent (although it does offer a silent *s* as compensation). Whatever you do, don't call it "bocce" to a Frenchman's face, even though it's almost exactly the same game, but played with hollow metal instead of solid wooden balls; hundred-year European wars have been started over less.

The courts are managed by La Boule New Yorkaise, and despite the fact that I'm a New Yorker studying French, this is the first time I've encountered the term *New-Yorkaise.* That's what they call New Yorkers in France? I thought it described how we talked. Anyway, seeing that my retirement "package"—and I should really mention this plan to Anne one of these days—includes playing *boules* and exchanging gossip every morning in whichever picturesque French village I retire to, I figure I should start practicing the game now. As I arrive, an eighty-year-old who, I learn, emigrated from France fifty years ago, has just finished setting up the courts. I tentatively ask the old gent for a game, and he's happy to oblige—oblige the way a shark agrees to babysit a young mackerel.

"You have played a lee-tle before maybe?"

"No," I say, not wanting even to mention bocce.

"In zat case, do you play for money?" He laughs at his own joke.

I don't, and good thing. Having grown up with backyard bocce at every family barbecue, I thought I knew my way around this game, but this guy is good, *pétanque*'s answer to Minnesota Fats. I never learn his name because, even though we're in an American park, this court is clearly French turf, and I've read that in France it is rude to ask someone his name.

This may be French turf, but Minnesota le Gros resists every attempt of mine to converse in French on it. I was hoping maybe I could kill two *oiseaux* with one *boule,* but I've run into a phenomenon I've experienced before: French immigrants, many of whom have worked hard to assimilate, don't particularly want to speak French, at least not to me. I persist anyway, testing a phrase here or there, as he—*grrrr*—replies in English, but my ego gets the best of me, and I soon abandon trying to drag any French out of him. Besides, I feel especially self-conscious speaking French to a Frenchman, even one who is not reluctant, and not so much because I know I speak it poorly. The real problem for Americans and Brits, according to some linguists, is that the phonemes of French, with its rolled *r*'s and nasal intonations, sound so silly to us that when we pronounce them properly we feel like we're doing an Inspector Clouseau parody, so we shy away from the correct pronunciations.

I need to focus not on French but on *pétanque,* anyway, as Minnesota le Gros keeps the first game close, close enough for me to want a second game, and is generous with advice. It is a nice way to learn the game, I'm thinking, in this low-pressure setting so reminiscent of France, playing with an actual and quite *gentil* Frenchman. Until something unexpected happens. A passerby stops to watch. Then another passerby notices that someone else has stopped to look at something—a squirrel, a mugging, a rolling ball, it doesn't matter—so he comes over to see what's happening. Well, with two people watching now, there must be something really big going on, so others stop to watch—the surest way to attract a crowd in New York is to start a crowd—and the next thing I know, my very first *pétanque* game is an exhibition in Bryant Park!

I personally would never stop to watch a *pétanque* match, but in France *pétanque* is a spectator sport, with championship play staged in large arenas and broadcast on TV. I've seen it on TV5Monde, and it's about as exciting as watching pigeons roost, with half the playing time devoted to players huddling around the balls, arguing over whose ball is closer, and most of the other half to their studying the layout and swinging their arms back and forth a dozen times before finally letting the ball loose, like nervous golfers on a putting green.

Le Gros notices the crowd and shifts into a higher gear, taking a 5–0 lead, although I'm in position to take 3 points and get back in the game. The object of *pétanque,* as with bocce, is to get as many of your balls closer to the little target ball, called a *cochonnet*—"piglet," for some reason—than your opponent does, and you score a point for each ball that is closer than the closest of your opponent's balls. By some stroke of fortune I've just placed my three *boules* reasonably close to the piglet, and as the crowd gathers, Le Gros crouches low with the third and last ball, his eighty-year-old knees nearly scraping the ground.

Then without warning his metallic ball is flying through the air in a shallow arc, catching the sunlight, back-spinning like crazy, looking like a silver orb circling the earth. It strikes the piglet right between the eyes, making a *crack* that reverberates around the park, sending piggy—and itself—back to where the shark's other two balls are. Score: Minnesota 8, *moi* 0. The crowd murmurs appreciatively at this amazing feat. I end up losing 13–0.

"*Ah, vous avez fait fanny!*"—you made fanny—Fats says with glee. So, that's how you get a Franco-American to speak French: make him crow!

"*Fanny? Qu'est-ce que c'est, fanny?*" I never miss a chance to ask the question *Qu'est-ce que c'est?* or its even better variant *Qu'est-ce que c'est que ça?* for the confounding-looking phrase rolls off the tongue, is easy to pronounce (no *r*'s!), and sounds very French. But most of all I fancy that the literal translation of the simple question "What's that?" is "What is this that this is that that?" And that *qu'est-ce que c'est* is repeated to great effect in the chorus of the Talking Heads hit "Psycho Killer."

Fats, returning to English, explains one of the more fascinating traditions of *pétanque:* the loser of a 13–0 shutout has to kiss the bare bottom of a girl named Fanny. For real. In twenty-first-century France, Fats notes with some disgust, a pictorial representation is usually substituted for the real thing—apparently it is not uncommon to see a fanny poster nailed to a tree at a *boulodrome*—either because no one is named Fanny anymore (could *pétanque* possibly be the reason why?) or because it was suspected that Frenchmen were throwing matches in order to get a smooch with Fanny's ass.

"No time for Fanny," I say, realizing with a bit of panic just how true that is. I rush to the doctor's office, breathlessly arriving two minutes before my appointment, only to wait two hours before being seen. I could've gotten a couple more fannies in.

IT DOESN'T TAKE THREE minutes with Dr. Larry Chinitz to realize you're talking to a very smart guy, possessing that kind of self-assuredness that surgeons often wear like a suntan (and he's got a pretty good one of those as well). I normally don't take to such people, but confidence is exactly what you want if the guy's going to be turning your heart into a shooting gallery. There is a potential cure for my condition, a procedure called radiofrequency catheter ablation, Chinitz explains, during which several catheters are snaked up from the groin into the heart via the blood vessels. Once inside, they hunt around for several hours like long-necked alien robots from science fiction movies (my analogy, not his), twisting, turning, probing for the "hot spots" that are causing the arrhythmia, which they then cauterize with radiofrequency energy.

I listen dumbly as Chinitz explains the procedure. This is not exactly a stroll along the Seine. "And it usually fixes the AFib? Forever?" I ask.

"Usually. In a few cases, especially if you've been in arrhythmia for a long time, a second ablation is required. But one generally does the trick."

"Risks?"

Complications, which occur in 2 to 3 percent of cases, range from bleeding at the groin to stroke. "But these tend to be in older or less healthy patients. Someone like you should expect a good outcome."

Yeah, well, someone like me ought to be speaking French by now, too. Which I decide to bring up, even though the appointment is running long and there are people in his packed waiting room who look like they've been there since the Restoration.

"Learning French is surprisingly stressful," I explain, on my way to asking if in his medical opinion I should quit, not sure of the answer I want to hear.

Before I can get there, this bilingual heart surgeon who earns his living *inside* other people's hearts says, "It is?" raising his eyebrows, and I feel foolish. "I'd think it would be fun."

"Oh, it is! There's something very soothing, even meditative, about putting on the headphones every morning and just getting lost in French for an hour. But it's just so much harder than I expected. I can't remember the silly words; it's so complicated, with all these dumb endings, and the pronunciation is impossible—and when I have to speak to anyone, I feel like a fool." I tell him how my initial AFib episode came on the heels of a difficult online class, and he smiles.

Chinitz, I learn, does not subscribe to the school of thought that atrial fibrillation is caused by stress, anxiety, moderate alcohol use (except in a very few sensitive individuals), caffeine, or French. He apparently hasn't used Rosetta Stone. What I neglected to mention in my soliloquy on the transcendent mornings of French is that they are punctuated by periods of sheer frustration. I almost threw my laptop out the window the other day because the Rosetta speech recognition engine would not accept my pronunciation of some simple sentence, no matter what twist I gave it. This meant I couldn't advance to the next screen; I was stuck, held hostage by my bad accent. My frustration mounted as the minutes ticked by, my heart pounding, and work beckoning.

I went into the program settings and changed the voice recognition sensitivity from moderate to easy. Still no luck. I resorted to screaming at the computer, hurling insults, French and English, until one of them—too crude to repeat here—apparently sounded close enough to the sentence it wanted that, to my utter amazement, the next screen popped up. Either that or I'd intimidated the program into submission. Or worn it out.

Which would be fair game, as French is wearing me out, although not as much as my heart troubles. So why not *ouvre mon cœur* up to Dr. Chinitz? Because, for one thing, I'm *peureux*—chickenhearted. The risk Chinitz cited sounds high to me, not low. Look at it this way: would you board a plane that, you were told beforehand, had a 2 to 3 percent chance of "complications"?

For another thing, I'm worried about the effect of hours of anesthesia on my brain. What if I wake up and find that I've forgotten what little French I've learned? Or worse, some of the English? My memory, which was bad to begin with (remember my abysmal cognitive-testing scores) is getting worse, and the harder I study French, the worse it seems to get.

"THE SUGAR?" ANNE ASKS a couple of days later, standing over a half-finished peach pie. I've just come back from the grocery store with the chicken, the potato chips, and the milk, but not the sugar, the main reason I went to begin with.

"I'm sorry. I have to start writing things down. I guess the longest mental list I can keep in my head is three items."

The previous evening, I had made dinner for guests, a pasta dish I've made dozens of times and have well committed to memory. Or had. "I also left out the egg last night," I muse aloud. "I thought maybe that learning French might make me smarter, but I'm turning into the village idiot."

Anne stops what she is doing and taps me gently on the forehead, leaving a spot of flour. "There's only so much room in there," she says. "Let me show you." She tilts her head far to the right as if trying to get water out of her ear and moves a pointed index finger toward her raised left ear. "French in!" Then she mimes something coming out of the other ear with her right index finger. "Oops! Egg out!"

She straightens up. "*¿Entiendes?*"

Yes, I understand, although I do wish she'd stop speaking Spanish. And I also wonder whether the great French experiment might be about over, whether it's time to throw in the towel, or as the French would say, *c'est la fin des haricots*! (It's the end of the beans!) Memory loss, heart rhythm loss . . . and I do wonder whether my heart worries are contributing to my inability to focus on French. Not only is it "French in, egg out"; lately it's been "French in, *French* out." I complain to Anne, "It seems that for every new word I learn, I forget a previous one. Moreover, as the lessons progress, the new words are getting more and more obscure. So I know the word for 'crutches'—and God help me if I ever need to know the French word for 'crutches'—but I've forgotten how to say 'next.' 'Next'! This is absurd; the more French I study, the less *useful* French I know!"

"Your brain is saturated," she says. "There's no more room."

"Well, I have to make some room." This conversation is starting to sound eerily familiar. The connection comes to me. "Sherlock Holmes."

"Huh?"

"In the very first Sherlock Holmes story, 'A Study in Scarlet,' Watson is astounded to learn that Holmes is unaware of Copernicus's discovery three hundred years earlier that the earth revolves around the sun. And Holmes says something like, 'What the deuce is it to me whether the earth revolves around the sun or the other way around? The mind is like an attic, with a finite amount of space, and a fool fills it up with every piece of junk he comes across, so it soon gets filled up and he can't uncover the important stuff that's up there. But a wise man only brings in the materials and tools that are of the most use to him.'" (I was a Sherlock Holmes geek as a child.)

Is my brain maxed out? Have I really reached the point of French in, French out? Or do I just need a furniture arranger, an interior decorator for my attic-brain? As it turns out, one is about to show up.

THE HISTORY OF MEMORY is generally dated to the legendary story related by Cicero about a tragic incident that occurred back in the fifth century BC. The Greek poet Simonides of Ceos was attending a banquet, the story goes, and had just stepped outside to have a smoke or take a phone call or something, when the palace collapsed, killing everyone inside, leaving the corpses so crushed under tons of stone that identification of the victims was impossible. One could not even say for sure who was inside. Families rushed to Simonides, asking if their loved ones were among the victims.

"How the hell should I know?" he might've said (except that the concept of hell was still a few centuries off), for he certainly hadn't taken attendance or even paid much attention. Yet, in the desperation of the moment, Simonides did a creative and unique thing. He closed his eyes and rebuilt the palace in his head, replaying his entrance and exit through the hall, *visualizing* the scene—"Ah, I nodded hello to Pseudolus on the way in, and remember wondering, how did he get a date with that cute Philia"—and re-creating in his mind's eye the seating arrangements. In this manner he was able to recall a remarkable number of those in attendance.

This event is the origin of the memorization technique known today, with a nod to Simonides, as the memory palace, a familiar room (or village or route) in which you strategically place the items you are memorizing. The Romans called it the method of loci (*loci* being Latin for "places"), and you may also hear it referred to as the peg system, for in one variant you hang the objects you are trying to remember on pegs in a familiar place.

The memory palace seems to be most effective when, instead of imaging the mundane object you are trying to remember, you substitute something related but more outrageous that will recall the object. Joshua Foer, who used the system to become the United States memory champion, gives the example of having to memorize a long shopping list that includes a snorkel and cottage cheese. He constructs his palace in his home, but instead of placing the snorkel on, say, the kitchen counter, he visualizes a man snorkeling in his kitchen sink, a much more bizarre—and therefore memorable—image. For the cottage cheese, he summons up Claudia Schiffer swimming in a vat of cottage cheese.

Memory techniques were in vogue in ancient times, before the advent of the written word, when possessing a sound memory was crucial, not only for shopping lists, but for *everything*. There is no question that the ancients had better memories than we do today. Without their extraordinary memories we'd have no *Iliad* or *Odyssey*, then or now. When the first writing systems appeared, there was much hand-wringing over what some saw as the inevitable demise of memory—a debate reawakened in the Internet age, when once again we are worrying about whether memory will become a sort of vestigial organ. After all, why memorize something when you can google it from your smartphone?

As writing reached the masses, the teaching of formal memory techniques fell out of fashion, but after hearing an interview with Foer, I wonder whether using the memory palace could help me with my French. Initially I'd thought not, because the operative word here is *learning*. That is, I am learning a language, not memorizing a few dozen handy phrases (*Où sont les toilettes?*) of the kind often supplied in guidebooks.

Well, a little research reveals that some linguists have indeed been promoting (and, naturally, others deriding) a mnemonic approach to learning foreign vocabulary for at least the past thirty years. Called the keyword method, this technique is a simple two-step process: Step one, take the foreign word and think of an English word (the keyword) that sounds like the foreign word. Step two, form an image in your mind that links the foreign and English words. For example, say you are trying to memorize the French word for "bread," *pain* (pronounced something like "pah"). This is close to "pan." So visualize a pan. Now picture that pan coming out of the oven filled with bread, and concentrate on that image for a few seconds. Bake it into your brain. Now, the next time you see the French word *pain,* you should be able to conjure up this picture, and say, "Aha, bread!"

How is this any better than simply memorizing that *pain* means "bread"? For the same reason that Simonides's memory palace technique works: the mind is remarkably adept at remembering images, but not so good at retaining words. In fact, the average adult can remember a list of only seven items (my own limit, as we have seen, is closer to three). It makes sense, evolutionarily speaking, that humans are better at remembering images than they are at remembering words, since we acquired sight way, way before we developed speech, not to mention writing. For that reason, various forms of visualization constitute the primary technique employed by all contemporary memory experts. The most common technique for memorizing the order of a deck of playing cards (a classic memory competition event) is to substitute a vivid image for each of the fifty-two cards in a deck.

Simple enough. Some months earlier I'd bought, and tried to memorize, an English-French children's dictionary of a thousand simple words. I never got past *C*. I retrieve the book and start again, this time using the mnemonic keyword technique. For *se plaindre* (to complain), I picture a bunch of talking *plantains* complaining about me every time I walk by. Funny. One word that has evaded me for weeks is *autoriser*, a verb meaning "to give permission." I close my eyes and picture myself in my mechanic's garage asking him for permission to put my car on his lift—his *auto riser*. Bingo. Ten minutes later, I test myself with a handful of new words, and pass. But as I add words, I start forgetting earlier words. It seems there is, as Anne (and Sherlock) had surmised, only so much room in there. My attic-brain is overfilled, bursting at the rafters.

To my dismay, though, two objects that seem to have taken up permanent residence—and precious room—in the attic are the snorkeler in my kitchen sink and poor Claudia Schiffer, still stuck in that vat of cottage cheese. I mean, I just can't get these images, which I'd had no intention of memorizing, out of my head. At the same time, I've forgotten the past tense of "to have." Clearly, Claudia is trying to tell me something. There *must* be a way to use the memory palace with French. I return to my English-French children's dictionary, opening it at the bookmarked letter *C,* and, covering the French translation, look at the word "coat." Damn, I had that word in seventh grade, again in high school, while prepping for French trips, and once again just a few months ago, not to mention the last time I was on this very dictionary page. But I still haven't learned it.

Okay, I'm going to build a memory palace and stick a coat in it. But where? I move my hand to reveal the translation: *manteau.* Borrowing from the keyword method of association, I first connect it to *mantel.* Then, constructing a memory palace, I place the coat on the fireplace mantel in my living room. *Mantel/manteau.* Good match, but a coat on a mantel is not very memorable. So let's put a man inside the coat and give him a hat, a *chapeau.* Ah, he just became a British *chap.*

Any well-dressed British chap up on a mantel needs an umbrella, that wonderful French word *parapluie,* which can double as a *para*chute if he needs to jump off. His wife, an unfortunate, homeless *bag* lady, wears a diamond *bague* on her finger. This couple's daughter is *jump*ing rope in her skirt (*jupe*), *impermeable* to the rain that's falling onto her yellow *imperméable.* As kids are wont to do, she is *pull*ing constantly at the sleeve of her sweater (*pull*).

But what is this strange crew doing in my living room? Sadly, it's a wake for the son, a ten-year-old kid, laid out in a *casket* wearing a baseball cap (*casquette*) and sneakers (*baskets*) under a *basket*ball hoop. I run through the scene with this odd family, whom I'm starting to enjoy, a few times in my head, jot down some notes, and test myself an hour later. Still there. The next day, the next *week*, still there. Thus it seems that while the key-word method itself doesn't work and the memory palace doesn't even really apply (it's usually employed to memorize mere lists of items), combining the two methods—assigning a keyword and placing that object in a palace—clicks! Of course, a week is one thing, but the big question remains: Will the French Addams family still be jumping rope in my living room during a wake in the rain next month, or next year, or will they have gotten bored and left? My guess is that to keep them there, I'll have to visit often.

Well, how many words can one memorize with this method? For starters, how about I try the thousand words in my children's English-French dictionary? Returning to the letter *A,* I divide the words that I don't know into themed rooms. The first room I build is an action room, for verbs. Nothing says "action" like a gym, so for this room I choose my former health club. As I enter, I see a strongman bench-*press*ing in a hurry (*être pressé*), while another athlete fills up (*remplir*) a water bottle to *replen*-ish his thirst, and so on. The next day, I'll revisit the gym, along with what has turned out to be my clothing-themed room (the Addams family), and begin the construction of my adjective room (the reading room of the New York Public Library), then a weather and outdoors room (the beach—it doesn't have to be a real room), and more.

When I need to retrieve a word, I simply go to the appropriate room and conjure up the right character. I review these lists nightly, and at some point I realize I've stopped using the keyword. I don't need to see the boy lying in a casket to recall the *casquette* on his head anymore, but the association is there if I need it.

When I've built and populated all my rooms, I give myself a test, running through the entire thousand-word dictionary from *A* to *Z*. My score: 98.5 percent. In ten days, not ten weeks or ten months, I've memorized virtually the entire *Mon premier Bescherelle anglais*!

STILL UNDECIDED ABOUT SURGERY, I worry that a few hours of anesthesia could sweep clean not only my carefully constructed memory palace rooms but some far more critical rooms—say, the ones in which I have my kids' names and where I live. And then there's that small percentage of complications, which I've magnified with my plane analogy. Still, if there's a good chance that a single procedure could fix my heart, could get that balky left atrium beating regularly again, why would I pass that up? "I'm only fifty-seven," I tell Anne.

"Fifty-eight."

During what verb conjugation did that happen? "Fifty-eight.

Do I really want to spend the rest of my life running on three cylinders?"

Anne thinks for a moment, and the physician in her replies, "Actually, it's two." Both atria are fibrillating.

The French have a saying: *Le cœur qui soupire n'a pas ce qu'il désire.* The heart that sighs does not have what it desires. In the morning I book a seat on Chinitz's plane, which doesn't depart for another few weeks. And distract myself by trying to focus on French.

Et Tu, Brute?

. . . .

The tu is generally used to insult a fellow automobilist
and always used when talking to oneself or to death.
—*International Herald Tribune,* February 19, 2000

"Yes, Bill, you can *tutoyer*."

Woo-hoo! My twenty-something glam-rocker part-time-model French pen pal, Sylvie, has given me the green light to use the familiar *tu* form with her. I feel *très français*.

Following protocol, or my understanding of protocol, I had first formally asked permission to use the familiar *tu*, and trust me, I agonized over the timing of this a good deal, because, well, a negative answer ("I think it's a little premature for that, Bill") would've been nothing short of humiliating. So I exhaled in relief when I received her reply, although something a little more positive, say, "Of course!" or "By all means—I thought you'd never ask!" would've been preferable to an answer that could just as easily be read as "[Sigh] If you must."

Even most non-Francophones know that the French use two pronouns for addressing a second person. That is, there are two ways to say "you": the formal (or polite) *vous* and the familiar *tu*. When to use which can be baffling to a foreigner, although to be fair to the French, they didn't make this business up. Blame the Latin that Julius Caesar brought to Gaul and that formed the basis of modern French. Thus it should come as no surprise that variations of *tu* and *vous* are also found in the other Romance languages, such as Italian, Spanish, and Romanian. Now, I don't know how it's handled in, say, Romania, or even other francophone countries, but in France the usage of *vous* and *tu* is less about grammar than about social position and how one views oneself and one's place in the world.

When I say that Caesar brought the formal *vous* to France, that's not strictly true. In the Latin of Caesar's day, everyone from your emperor to your dog was just *tu*. The Latin *vos* was strictly reserved for the plural ("you all"). The use of *vos* (which would become the French *vous*) to refer to a single person didn't appear until the fourth century, and came about almost by accident. Its first use was to refer only to the dual Roman emperors, both of them, because by then the empire had split into an eastern empire ruled from Constantinople and a western empire overseen from Rome. Politically, however, the two emperors ruled with one joint voice, and to hammer home the point they began to refer to themselves as *nos,* or "we." (This may be the origin of the royal "we" that today one tends to associate with English queens.)

Once the inevitable confusion that must have resulted was cleared up—I have this image of the western emperor sitting alone on his throne telling a puzzled page, "We'd like some coffee," and the page returning with two cups and being called an idiot—the emperors' people had to deal with a touchy issue of protocol: how to address someone who refers to himself as "we." They wound up deciding that if the emperor was going to refer to himself in the plural, they'd damn well better address him likewise, so they began to address each individual emperor in the plural, *vos.*

So far, so good. But the next thing you knew, the pope was demanding parity (there is written evidence of Gregory I referring to himself in the plural in the late sixth century), and this *vos* thing started to mean something other than a double-headed emperor; it had become an honorific title bestowing status. Kings started insisting on being addressed as *vos,* then nobles, and then not-so-nobles, as the custom filtered, top-down, through the social strata of Europe, until it reached the point where French peasants had their children calling them *vous.* Naturally, people who expected to be addressed as *vous* reciprocally addressed that person as *tu.* This is what linguists call the power semantic: the use of *tu* and *vous* to convey superior (or concede inferior) power or status.

Well, what about people of the same social stratum? What

were they to call one another? Back in the good old days, everyone was just *tu,* but now with all these power games going on, a new set of rules was needed. The upper crust considered themselves the elite and referred to one another as *vous,* even husbands and wives. Peers of the lower classes, meanwhile, stuck with *tu,* often as a point of pride, a show of solidarity, a syntactic sneer at the upper classes. For that reason, the reciprocal usage of *tu* or *vous* among people of similar classes is called the solidarity semantic.

The French nearly managed to do away with all this during the French Revolution, with the Committee for Public Safety condemning the usage of *vous* as a feudal vestige. Robespierre even addressed the president of the Assembly as *tu,* an act that could've bought you a ticket to the guillotine just a few months earlier. But cooler heads—or rather, warmer heads, those still attached to bodies—prevailed, and as republican ideals went out the window in the Restoration that followed, *vous* was restored along with the Crown.

A scenario similar to the events of 1789 played out during the May 1968 student uprisings, when protestors, like the *sans-culottes* of two centuries earlier, threw off the shackles of the oppressive *vous,* although as they have aged and entered the workplace and mainstream society, many have lost their *tutoyer* principles along with their long hair. Meanwhile, although we no longer address waiters as *tu* and expect them to call us *vous,* it is still common to have such a relationship with your boss at work or your teacher in school. In the 2008 French movie *The*

Class, a student is dragged to the principal's office for having committed the offence of using *tu* with a teacher.

The solidarity semantic is going strong as well. If anything, the lines between *vous* and *tu* have blurred and the unwritten rules have become more inscrutable. Take, for example, my dilemma with Sylvie: At what point does someone become enough of an intimate to be called *tu*? And for that matter, who makes the first move? Not to worry: the French have developed an entire formal protocol for how it's done, even going so far as to invent a verb (*tutoyer*) that means "to address each other with the *tu* form."

Here's how it works: When you first meet someone, you generally address each other as *vous,* unless your relationship comes under one of the three dozen or so overriding rules (adult/child, etc.). You and your new acquaintance might see each other again and continue chatting, even have a coffee together. And at some point, when it feels right, one of you will say to the other some variation of *On se tutoie?* meaning, "Shall we use the *tu* form with each other?" And with any luck the other will agree.

Gulp. To me, this little mating dance holds all the risks and none of the rewards of asking a girl to the senior prom, a prospect I found so terrifying that I confess I never actually got around to it. Indeed, I felt my gut tightening when I asked Sylvie "*On se tutoie?*" via e-mail. What gave me the courage to try was Sylvie's use of the intimate greeting, "*Coucou,* Bill!" in her recent notes.

Coucou? When I told her in my response that my dictionary

defined it as a bird or a clock, she explained, "It is like the American word 'hi,' it's very familiar and mostly used for friends and family :)" Okay, I figured, I've made it to *tutoyer*-ville, especially with that smiley she tacked on (which raises a whole other set of questions about the relationship of emoticons and the formal second person, which I am not prepared to go into here, or anywhere, or ever), and the time seemed right to, well, propose.

Now, had I been more familiar with these protocols, I would've known that because I'm old enough to be Sylvie's father, I should've used the *tu* form with her from the get-go. She, on the other hand (had she been writing in French, not English), would properly have called me *vous,* which would have been more than a little weird, a reminder in every sentence that "you're old enough to be my father," so I in turn would have invited her to *tutoyer.* This is ignoring the fact, of course, that the Internet, informal by nature, must have its own set of rules. *Oy vey!*

IT'S DATE NIGHT IN the Alexander household, meaning a French dinner that includes my to-die-for *pommes Anna**

---

* Slice 4 potatoes very thinly on a mandoline. Clarify 4 tablespoons of sweet butter by melting and skimming off the milk solids that float to the surface. Layer potatoes with plenty of salt and pepper and the clarified butter into an 8-to-10-inch oven-safe, nonstick pan. Cover with foil and cook on stovetop over high heat for 90 seconds. Transfer to 425-degree oven and bake for 45 minutes, removing foil after 30. Place platter on top and flip, like an upside-down cake.

(the only dish I know of that's named after a prostitute—you can look it up), followed by a well-reviewed French movie I've picked out, in turn followed, with any luck, by a little French kissing.

We'll have to do our smooching in English because, remarkably, the French do not have a term for "French kissing." I mean, nothing at all! Therefore the 2014 *Petit Robert* dictionary, perhaps concerned about the impact this might be having on the already low French birthrate, has just proposed one—a very odd concept for Americans, who kind of just wait for a new word to arrive naturally—coming up with the verb *galocher,* which is derived from the word for an ice-skating boot, the idea apparently being that a French kiss is kind of sliding around on the ice, but with your lips and tongue. Okay. You can like it or hate it, but as we know, *Petit Robert* is not the final arbiter. What I wouldn't give to be in the room when the Académie française takes this up!

Back at date night, we were up to the French movie part. It's been my observation that about 90 percent of French films fall roughly into one of just two plotlines. The first is of the man-loves-woman-loves-another-man-loves-another-woman variety, with luscious scenery and exquisitely worn scarves.

The second category consists of movies that leave you despairing about the futility of existence, the folly of love, and how the hell you could have chosen this movie for date night! Tonight's feature, *Les herbes folles* (*Wild Grass*), by the acclaimed director Alain Resnais, belongs, regrettably, to this group. Everyone ends up dead in the end, including, I suspect, no small number of viewers who watched it all the way through, but it isn't a total loss because of a didactic moment that crystallizes for me just how powerful, and meaningful, this *tu* business is.

Georges, who is about sixty, is opening a bottle of champagne, surrounded by his wife, daughter, and son-in-law, Jean-Mi, who has apparently been in the family for some time, long enough to have given Georges two grandchildren. As everyone sips champagne, and the laughter and good times roll, Jean-Mi figures the moment is right for the *tutoyer* gambit.

JEAN-MI: We could use *tu* now.

GEORGES: I'd rather not, if you don't mind. Do you mind?

JEAN-MI: No, no, I was just asking.

GEORGES: Use *tu* to say what? We're fine like this, aren't we?

At which point I turn to Anne and say, "Wow, now *that's* using the power semantic!"

She says, "How much longer do we have to watch this?"

"But this is amazing! They're having a whole discussion on *tutoyer*! We have *nothing* like this in America!"

"No, sir, we don't."

"Cute."

But outside the military and the South, even "sir," which, of course, isn't quite the same thing, has become rare. However, I did get an intriguing lesson in how things might have turned out had American English retained a version of *vous/tu* when during my first hospital stay I read, in French (with the help of a dictionary and a translation), the 1946 Jean-Paul Sartre play *The Respectful Prostitute,* which takes place in America's Deep South. The play opens with a knock at the door and a man addressing a prostitute with *vous,* while she returns a *tu.* This confused me greatly. Who would be addressing a hooker in the formal, while receiving the familiar?

A *Noir,* or a black man, that's who. (As it happens, in a few decades Mexicans will appear on the scene and an American *Noir* will have someone to call *tu.*) By the way, you might expect that a prostitute, on the (almost) lowest rung of society's ladder, would use *vous* to address the man who appears later in the scene, her distinguished and wealthy client, but in fact they address each other as *tu.* There's a saying in Spanish that "prostitutes are women who smoke and treat you with *tú.*" It makes sense, if you think about what you're really paying for.

By the way, *tu* is not forever. Should the need arise to go back to *vous*—say, if you catch your best friend in bed with your wife—the French, bless 'em, who didn't have a word for "French kiss" until ten minutes ago, do have a word you can use here: *vouvoyer.*

WHAT MAKES THIS ALL so difficult is that there are no hard-and-fast rules. In a piece published in the *International Herald Tribune,* the English-language newspaper based in Paris,

Mary Blume wrote that foreigners "cannot hope to master the intricacies of the *tu* and *vous* forms of address, because the French can't either." Still, I've been able to glean some rules, which I've put into a simple flowchart (see next page) that I recommend you take with you on your next trip to France.

SO HOW DID WE English speakers manage to avoid this curse? After all, English is the offspring of Old French and German, another language that has formal and familiar terms of address (*Sie* and *du,* respectively). In fact, for a while English did have both forms, but unlike gender, which vanished entirely, vestiges of the formal and familiar are still found today, mainly in church, where "thou" is frequently used in prayer, but not, as you might think, as a formal, respectful way of addressing God. Quite the opposite: "thou" is the early modern English equivalent of *tu;* it is "ye" that corresponds to *vous.* (Speaking of God, in the French translation of the Bible, everyone just calls everyone else *tu.* Apparently, French Jesus does not expect his disciples to *vouvoyer* him, even as they refer to him as "Master.")

By the seventeenth century, "thou" was falling into disuse, even becoming a form of contempt, used the way the French might pointedly *tutoyer* a rude shopkeeper or a dishonest mechanic. Certainly no one living in England in 1603 would have missed the highly insulting use of the term in Sir Edward Coke's famous attack on Sir Walter Raleigh: "I thou thee, thou

. . . .

A Short Guide to Using *Vous* and *Tu*

. . . .

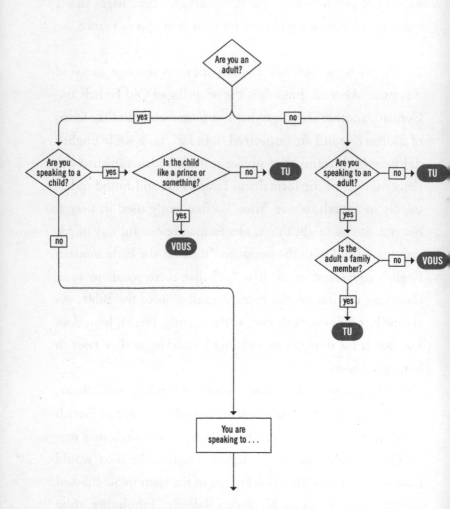

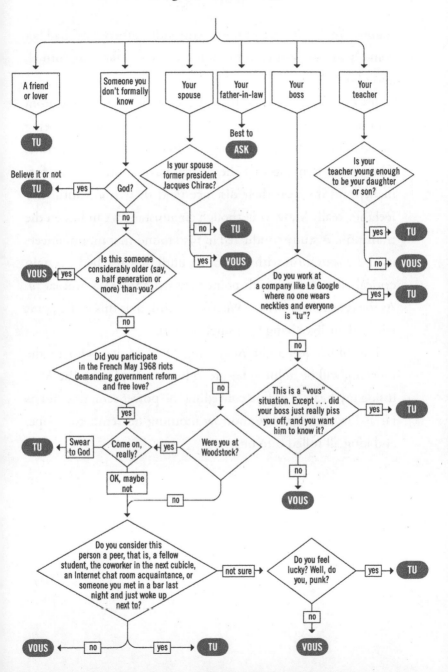

traitor!" Yet by the end of the seventeenth century, "ye" had become "you" and was used to address everyone: familiar, formal, and plural.

It's interesting to note that just as "thou" was fading from common usage in English, the Académie française was being founded to codify such things in France. *Vive la différence!* There is no denying that the French have a fondness for formality and do keep their distance (and their *vous*) until they feel they really know you, though circumstances can hasten the transition. A study conducted in 1950 found that mountaineers used the *vous* form with each other until they reached a certain critical altitude, at which point they switched to a mutual *tu*. As the researchers write, "We like to think that this is the point where their lives hang by a single thread."

I wouldn't feel right *tutoyer*-ing Dr. Chinitz, who in the morning will be holding *my* life in his hands, playing Pac-Man inside my heart. I'm fine conceding the power semantic, for as far as I'm concerned, tomorrow morning he's emperor, pope, and king all rolled into one.

Baby Jesus in Velvet Shorts

. . . .

In Paris they simply stared when I spoke to them
in French; I never did succeed in making those idiots
understand their own language.

—MARK TWAIN

"*Vingt, dix-neuf, dix-huit . . .*" To see if I've made fanny—that
is, suffered any cognitive damage—during the procedure, the
first thing I do when stirred awake in the recovery room is to
start counting backward from twenty in French, a totally spon-
taneous, unpremeditated act that must've been subliminally
planted by the exercise in my Meetup.com class. Although it's
something I'm lucky to accomplish on my best days after two
cups of coffee, I make it to *zéro* and relax a bit.

"How do you feel, Mr. Alexander?"

I'm surprised to hear Dr. Chinitz use "mister" with me.
Maybe no one addresses you as *vous* in an American hospital,

but everyone does call you "mister," which is close enough. So even though I'm freezing, my back is absolutely killing me, my heart hurts (literally), and my mouth and throat feel like I've been gargling with ground glass, I mumble, "Great. How'd we do?"

"Just fine. You had quite a bit of activity in there, so we were in surgery a little longer than we'd planned."

"How long?"

"Eight hours." It's four in the afternoon.

Zut alors! No wonder my back is killing me. And I have to stay flat, without moving, for another excruciatingly long four hours, until the catheter entry points are clotted. Chinitz orders some pain meds and a heater for my death-rattle chill. The temporary discomfort, as great as it is, seems a small price to pay, for when I feel my heart singing *lubb-dupp, lubb-dupp,* for the first time in months, it's a *chanson*—the sweetest song I've ever heard.

I'M UNDER DOCTOR'S ORDERS to stay home and take it easy for a week, which solves a scheduling issue I've been having. A couple of weeks earlier, I'd received another *bonjour* from the language-networking site MyLanguageExchange, this one from a Frenchwoman who wants to skype (that is, talk), but with her job, my job, and the six-hour time difference, we hadn't been able to find a mutually good time—until now.

Catherine is a woman in her fifties living with her two dogs in the trendy Montmartre neighborhood so beautifully evoked in *Amélie,* the whimsical 2001 film that made Audrey Tautou an international star. We talk for over an hour, but Catherine, who is fluent in English, mainly just wants someone to talk to in English. I ask if we can speak in French. She says something unintelligible.

"*Répétez, plus lentement?*" I request.

She repeats, more slowly.

I still don't understand.

"How about you speak in English and I speak in French?" I suggest. We chat for a while in this way, and the French is coming with great difficulty and, I know, many, many errors. Catherine is quite happy to tell me, in very good English, about her day at work, what she's making for dinner, her horrible boss, and the weather in Paris, and while the cultural exchange is enjoyable, I'm trying to learn French, and this isn't helping *un morceau.* I ask her if she would be willing to correct my spoken errors. There is a long pause.

"If I correct every error," she says as politely as you can say something like this, "we cannot have a conversation."

Ouch. Well, the French are known for being direct. Nevertheless, that stinger will be sticking around in my attic-brain long after I've forgotten the first-person past tense of "to embarrass," that's for sure.

Meanwhile, while we've been burning up the wires chatting, Catherine has burned her dinner. I feel responsible and try to make up for it with an elegant good-bye: "*C'était un grand plaisir.*" *Now* she decides to correct me—specifically my pronunciation.

"*Plaisiirre,*" she says, drawing the word out so pleasurably, so sensually, it's like her tongue has reached across the Atlantic and is flicking my ear. It is the single most beautiful word in French I have ever heard, the perfect fusion of word and meaning, of form and function. "*Plaisiir,*" I try hopelessly to imitate.

She is not impressed. What am I doing wrong?

"You have to get into the mind of the culture," she explains. "Each language means one culture, one behavior, one emotion. So when I was young, learning English, I tried to feel English, by which I mean a little snobbish. When I learned Spanish, I made myself feel very proud. And German . . ." A pause. "German, you can imagine. But that was more my instinct than my intellect. Anyway, it has helped me; it is like to play as an actor. So I think it would help you to know how you feel the French and 'play' one of us. That's just an advice."

Damn good advice. When you hear that so-and-so has a gift for languages, you think of being able to remember vocabulary or having a good ear for pronunciation. But I'd never considered this intangible, the ability to connect to the culture, to pick up language clues and cues from the nature of the people speaking it. Perhaps this is the source of the "gift" for languages.

It's hard to "play as an actor" when using Rosetta Stone, which ignores culture totally in its one-photograph-fits-all-languages approach. In eight months with the course, I learned not a single thing about French customs, the French psyche, or even French cheese. But from a single conversation with Catherine, I've learned that they still think the English are haughty, the Spanish too proud, and as for the Germans—"you can imagine."

A few days later, searching for my inner Frenchman, I repaint the kitchen—in bright Provence yellow and blue. It's a start.

IN A BROADER SENSE, what—if anything—does a language tell us about its people? The myriad rules of conjugation and grammar would suggest the French like (and abide by) regulations, as anyone who's even just mailed a parcel in France can attest. Yet I would argue that it's the language's idioms, invented not by salons and committees but by common folk, that provide the clearest window into the French soul. Compare the American (in most cases, British as well) and French versions of these common idioms:

AMERICAN: It costs an arm and a leg
FRENCH: *Il coûte la peau du cul* (It costs the skin of the ass)

AMERICAN: Bottoms up!
FRENCH: *Cul sec!* (Dry ass!)

AMERICAN: To tie the knot
FRENCH: *Se passer la corde au cou* (To put a rope around your neck)

AMERICAN: To have a stroke of fortune
FRENCH: *Avoir le cul bordé de nouilles* (To have an ass full
of noodles)

AMERICAN: To have a wet dream
FRENCH: *Faire une carte de France* (To make a map of France)

In case you're as baffled as I initially was, that last one comes from the shape of the splotch of semen that a teenage boy might wake up with on his belly. (Mine was always more Italy, but close enough.) Asses, nooses, and geographic ejaculations! The French versions of these idioms are earthier, more rural, and more vulgar than anything an American would dream of saying. As are the French people. They in turn find us prudish, pointing to the fact that our public television stations don't even have a late-night porn channel. But look carefully at some of these idiomatic differences: certainly hanging a noose around a French groom's neck is *a far cry* (goodness, it's hard to write without using idioms) from his American cousin's tying the knot. Shall we discuss the notorious sexism of French society or the widespread custom of French men taking mistresses while we're at it?

For other idioms, it's just interesting to see the slight differences: We eat crow; they swallow grass snakes. We kick the bucket; they eat dandelions by the root (I love that one). To a Frenchman a condom is an English letter; to an Englishman it's a French letter—tit for tat, you might say (but the French would say *à bon chat, bon rat*—to a good cat, a good rat). We have a frog in the throat; they have a cat in the throat. We have other fish to fry; they have other cats to whip. We buy a pig in a poke; they buy a cat in a pouch. We call a spade a spade; the French call a cat a cat. Something about the French and cats, it seems. And while we're on felines, what we vulgarly call "pussy" the French call "cat"—*chatte*—and yes, it's a feminine *chat*. At least they got this one right (cf. "breasts" and "vagina").

I've saved the best for last. Surely the strangest idiom in this country renowned for its disdain for organized religion is one that a Frenchman might say after sipping a smooth red wine: *C'est le petit Jésus en culotte de velours!* It's the baby Jesus in velvet shorts!

What!?

Relax, it's just the French way of saying "It's the tops!" (a Roaring Twenties flapper might've said, "It's the cat's pajamas!") or it goes down easy, like God in velvet shorts—or underpants, depending on who's translating. You get the idea, although getting the idea doesn't make it any less curious. My secret fantasy is to see an American presidential candidate slip up and use that expression on the stump: "Winning Connecticut would be the baby Jesus in velvet shorts!" Not only would his career be over, but I swear, I'd probably make a map of France, right then and there.

French and the Middle-Aged Mind

· ·

Middle age is that perplexing time of life when we hear two voices
calling us, one saying, Why not? and the other, Why bother?
—SYDNEY J. HARRIS, American journalist (1917–1986)

On November 4, 1970, Los Angeles County authorities made
a gruesome discovery in the form of a teenage girl, given the
pseudonym of Genie, who had spent nearly her entire thirteen years isolated in a bedroom in her parents' house, strapped
most of that time to a potty chair, rarely touched, and never
played with or hugged—or spoken to. And because of her lack
of exposure to it, Genie had not acquired language, could not
even vocalize.

Her case sparked the interest of scientists around the world,
including Susan Curtiss, a first-year graduate student of linguistics at UCLA, who saw a rare opportunity to test the "critical period hypothesis." Proposed just three years earlier by

neurologist Eric Lenneberg, it stipulated that language could be acquired only during a window starting in late infancy and ending with the onset of puberty. The notion of a cutoff age (while Lenneberg put it at around twelve, most scientists today suggest an age closer to six) for acquiring language was almost as galvanizing in the linguistics community as Noam Chomsky's controversial theories a decade earlier.

Under Curtiss's tutelage, Genie began to acquire vocabulary at a rapid rate, "hungry to learn the words for all the new items filling her senses," Curtiss later wrote. Learning syntax, however, was another story. Even as Genie learned to speak, she remained stuck at the two-word-string stage ("Me hungry") for years, and when she used a third word, it was often out of order or meaningless ("Applesauce buy store"). Even after a full seven years of intensive language rehabilitation, Genie never acquired the ability to produce a negative sentence or ask a question, not even the persistent one-word question we most associate with toddlers: "Why?"

Genie, at the age of thirteen, was too old to acquire language.

Abused children make for poor research subjects, as do feral children,* but studies involving youngsters who acquire language—American Sign Language—at varying ages have

---

* Fans of French cinema will be familiar with François Truffaut's movie *The Wild Child,* based on the true story of a feral child, a boy who was discovered foraging for food outside a French village in 1800. The arc of his story is remarkably similar to Genie's; he, too, was not able to acquire language.

since lent credence to the idea of a critical period. The concept of a biologically based limit for acquiring language may seem counterproductive, but critical periods are quite common in the animal kingdom. Perhaps the closest parallel can be found among birds, who, if not exposed to their species' birdsong by a certain age, will never acquire it.

Why would nature have evolved critical periods? Steven Pinker, the Harvard psychologist, suggests that the brain—especially the young, developing brain—has a lot of work to do, and it can't do everything at once. Learning language (as opposed to *using* language) is pretty much a one-time proposition. It is, as Pinker puts it, "use it then lose it." Once you've acquired language, which metabolically is very expensive, you no longer need the scaffolding that has been set up for your brain in order to facilitate that function. Your body returns the language-acquisition set of genes to the gene library and checks out a different set, perhaps the ones you need to sense danger or kill a wild boar, to learn math, or to operate your iPad. Pinker writes, "The linguistic clumsiness of tourists and students might be the price we pay for the linguistic genius we displayed as babies."

The theory is backed up by the remarkable neurological changes going on in the young brain during the period when we are learning language. The newborn brain—the one that learns language before learning to tie its shoes—comes out of the womb with, give or take, 100 billion neurons, each connected to about 2,500 other neurons. As the brain develops during the first two to three years of life, the period when language acquisition is taking place, the neurons continue to make additional connections, or synapses, up to an average of 15,000 each (some neurons will make as many as 100,000 synapses).

This is way more than even the developing brain needs, but the redundancy has a purpose: Brains aren't perfect, and the plethora of synapses allows, for example, language function or vision to move from one region to another if there are problems. And there often are problems, starting with birth, when the soft skull is squeezed through the smaller opening of the mother's cervix. The surplus of synapses also allows the brain to adapt to the particular circumstances of its environment, a feature called plasticity. For example, if you are born blind (or are blinded early in life), the aural centers can develop more, compensating by providing you with especially acute hearing. Surrounded by not one but two spoken languages? The language centers grow.

Up to a point. Beginning at the age of two or three, the unused synapses start to get—in the surprising term that neurologists share with gardeners—pruned. The synapses that are in use (one might say, bearing fruit) stay, but the unused ones (including, in my case, those that might have been learning *français* while I was in the crib) start dropping like French soldiers under fire. By adulthood, you've got less than half the synapses you had before you were out of diapers. It's been theorized that these extra brain synapses are vital to the acquisition of language.

The neurology of language acquisition isn't fully understood, although the existence of a critical period is now nearly universally accepted. But what about learning a second language? I remember hearing references to a second-language critical period at the language conference I attended. Does such a thing truly exist? Is there a critical period for second-language acquisition?

I put that question to Elissa Newport, a cognitive scientist at the University of Rochester who has studied both first- and second-language acquisition. Newport is the coauthor, with Jacqueline Johnson, of a 1989 paper that studied forty-six Korean- and Chinese-born immigrants, ranging in age from three to thirty-nine. All had come to the United States with no prior knowledge of English, and all had been living in the States for comparable periods, with comparable exposure to English, being either students or teachers. Each subject was given a test consisting of a list of simple English sentences, half of them grammatically correct, and half containing errors such as "Yesterday the hunter shoots a deer." The subjects were asked to spot the incorrect sentences.

The immigrants who had arrived between the ages of three and seven performed identically to American students. Those who had arrived between eight and fifteen did increasingly worse the later they arrived. Those who'd arrived after age seventeen did the worst of all, but—here's the interesting part—in that older group, age was not strongly correlated to performance, and success seemed more closely tied to individual differences than to age. Thus a thirty-nine-year-old arrival could potentially perform as well as a twenty-five-year-old arrival—but neither adult could come close to the proficiency of a child who had immigrated at age twelve.

Newport and Johnson argued that this large drop-off in skill after late adolescence—the graph of the data resembles a slight decline followed by a cliff (not the linear decline I'd heard a speaker describe at the SLRF language conference)—was evidence of a biologically based critical period for second-language acquisition, comparable to the one for first language. Why should this happen? "The brain changes over life," Newport tells me over the phone. "It doesn't apply to everything. We can learn lots of things pretty well as adults, but certainly for language and I think for other skills sort of like language, the plasticity—the machine—just doesn't quite work as well." Neurological studies suggest, she says, that adult brains speaking a new language are doing something different from children's brains doing the same task. I wonder what my own brain will look like when I repeat the fMRI scans.

Plasticity aside, there's another reason why kids are so much better at learning language than adults. "Kids are assisted by the fact that they're so incompetent," Newport says, explaining her "less is more" theory. "They start out being able to pick up very, very few elements out of a very complicated stream of speech,

And that might seem like a disadvantage, but what it actually does, given the way human languages work, is it ends up directing them to the smaller bits, and the most prominent bits, to start with." Kids get the important stuff, like nouns and verbs, at the beginning, and they don't worry about the rest—like subject-verb agreement—and they get up and running with a basic command of the language quickly.

"But adults," Newport continues, "try to do everything. They're much more capable than kids are at pulling out and remembering bigger bunches of the speech stream to which they're exposed. And then they have to figure out how the hell they're organized." Or, to borrow from the title of one scholarly paper written on this topic, we grown-ups might just be "too smart for our own good."

If Newport and Johnson's claim of a true second-language critical period—which I've missed by about thirty years—is true, well, *c'est la fin des haricots*! I'm wasting my time. But the theory remains a divisive one among scientists, so to get another view I contact David Birdsong, a researcher and professor of linguistics at the University of Texas. Birdsong (best name for a linguist *ever*), while agreeing that "earlier is better," is skeptical of a sharp, biologically based critical period for second-language acquisition.

"I think the biology part is overstated," he tells me, postulating that it's the very existence of your *first* language, not some dramatic changes taking place in the brain at adolescence, that presents the main obstacle to learning a second language. "You've been speaking English for the past fifty-six or so years," he says. "Therefore, the second language is always going to be talking back and forth with the first. Whenever you say something in one language the other language is activated to some degree. L2ers listen through L1 ears." That is, you process your second language through the ears of your first. And the longer you've spoken your first language—meaning, the older you are—the more entrenched you've become in it and the harder it is to break free, whether we're talking about hearing the foreign language's phonemes or applying the rules of syntax.

The normal, gradual processes of aging are a hindrance as well. "Processing speed slows down with age, there's no question about it," he tells me. And processing speed is critical to language comprehension. While I'm still processing word *A*, the speaker has gone on to words *B, C,* and *D*. When you're familiar with a language, you don't process it word by word; you process it in chunks. As Birdsong explains, "You're able as an English processor to anticipate the next word that's coming out of my mouth. With French, or Chinese, or Spanish, nothing sounds familiar."

And as if that's not bad enough, "one of the things about French is that it doesn't give you a lot of cues as to where words begin and end. French is horrible this way. It doesn't lend itself to figuring out where boundaries between words and phrases are." To illustrate this using an example in English, it's really hard for even a native speaker without a context to discern whether someone is saying "the stuffy nose" or "the stuff he knows."

There are more challenges for the middle-aged language student. "We see a loss in word retrieval ability," says Birdsong. "When you're sixty years old, you can still learn a new word. You can learn *e-mail;* that word didn't exist that long ago. The ability to sort of 'bank' new items is simply not going away with age. What does go away with age—and this is a kicker—is your ability to come up with that item on demand." I'm quite familiar with that phenomenon as well—what I call my French vapor lock, when I just freeze up, unable to recall a word.

Birdsong doesn't reject the role of biology. Language acquisition, he tells me, is directly affected by the levels of both dopamine and acetylcholine, neurotransmitters that play critical roles in the brain in everything from cognition to emotion and that, like testosterone, decline with age. This was the last place in the world I expected to hear about my declining testosterone, but in fact, Birdsong sings, "The function of testosterone in language is undeniable. Word retrieval and rate of speech are highly dependent on testosterone levels at a given moment. So from morning to afternoon, rate of speech, word retrieval, and fluency can all be a function of testosterone level, in men *and* women."

In other words, learning French isn't just mental; it's

biological and hormonal as well. And the same hormone involved in sexual performance is giving me grief in learning French! I mean, really, who knew?

I take it all in: being too smart for my own good, loss of ability to detect unique French phonemes, first-language interference, loss of synapses, decrease in processing speed, and plummeting levels of dopamine, acetylcholine, and testosterone. It seems the odds are stacked against me. Heidi Byrnes had been so encouraging about using age to play to our strengths, our very maturity, but the science doesn't seem to be on my side. I ask Birdsong if there are any data on fifty-eight-year-olds acquiring a second language. Not a whit. Too many adult learners get discouraged and quit early on. Well, not this one, I tell Birdsong, who in response throws me a lifeline of hope. Look, he says, there's no denying that older people have a poor success rate in learning second languages, but what characterizes the late starters is the wide variability that is not seen among children. Some adult learners end up doing very well.

Even Elissa Newport, who started the brouhaha over the postulated existence of a second-language critical period, isn't ready to write me off.

"Do I have a fighting chance?" I ask her.

"Yeahhh!" she says encouragingly. "But honestly, I think you've got to live in the country."

By which she doesn't mean on a farm. Well, that's not about

to happen anytime soon, but the message I've taken away from both Newport and Birdsong is that learning French is certainly possible at my age, but difficult.

I'm going to have to turn it up a notch. There is, however, one other little issue vying for my attention, which is related not to my middle-aged mind but to my middle-aged body.

TWO WEEKS AFTER MY surgery, I feel a few rapid beats. They pass. They return. I try to will my heart back into rhythm, which is about as effective as willing my brain into understanding the French evening news on TV5Monde. With Anne safely at work, I come up with the creative idea that intentionally speeding up my heartbeat might break the AFib, so I start racing laps in the pool. Anne comes home to find me in AFib—and wet.

"You did what?" she says, incredulous. "What if you—" She can't bring herself to finish the sentence. "Have you called NYU?"

"I'm hoping it will break." The thought of going down there for another jolt is . . . well, I guess it's enough to have sent me alone into eight feet of water with a fibrillating heart. Anne hands me the phone.

"What'd they say?" Anne asks when I hang up.

"*Merde.*"

She doesn't laugh.

"Cardioversion tomorrow morning."

I'D THOUGHT THE EIGHT-HOUR surgery I'd endured was the end of my heart saga, but it turns out to have been only the preface. In the six weeks following the surgery, I'll be shocked out of AFib *three* more times, turning the Double-O brand above my heart into the Olympic rings, each jolt leaving my chest feeling like it's been struck by a battering ram.

I am as low as I have ever been, checking my pulse a hundred times a day, wondering whether each blip means another date with the DieHard, if not Jesus, and questioning the decision to have had the surgery in the first place. Finally, when I'm rushed to the hospital in the midst of my fourth postsurgery arrhythmia, my blood pressure resembling the score of a high school basketball game, Dr. Chinitz is waiting. His steady, dry hands grasp mine. "Let's get you fixed," he says. He nods to a nurse, and I'm wheeled into surgery for my second—and I trust my last—ablation.

RECUPERATING AT HOME A few days later, I'm cheered by a sweet e-mail from Sylvie.

> Hello Bill :)
> I can tell you that I was worried about you, for your heart!!! i hope and pray that your doctor get all the gremlins now and you have a new heart who will take the good rythm, the rock'n'roll rythm!!
> Friendly, Sylvie

Her note not only makes me laugh but prompts me to dwell on the likelihood that her grammatical error—"a new heart who" instead of "which"—stems from the fact that the French use the same word (*qui*) for both people and things, for "who" and "which." Finally, something that's simpler in French than in English! I put on the headphones and resume where I'd left off a few weeks ago, with the *passé composé*.

Merci, Sylvie.

Glazed and Confused

. . . .

"Je suis a stranger here," I said in flawless French.
"Je veux aller to le best hotel dans le town."
—F. SCOTT FITZGERALD,
"How to Live on Practically Nothing a Year," 1924

Six o'clock, Saturday evening. The elevator doors part, a woman steps out, and I enter the empty elevator. The woman stops suddenly, looking every bit as puzzled as if she'd just been dropped off on Mars, then looks plaintively to me for help.

"Not the lobby yet," I say. "Eleven."

"The eleventh floor? This is where I got on. I haven't moved!" She has been standing, unaware, for a full minute, in a closed but stationary elevator. I see the glazed look in her eyes and instantly understand. She recognizes the same punch-drunkenness in mine and laughs. "Language-immersion class?"

"French level two. You?"

"Level one."

This is French on the Go, the weekend immersion foreign language program run by the New School, formerly known as the New School for Social Research—aptly named, for by the time it's all over, I'll feel a bit like I've been a *subject* of social research, having spent Friday evening, all day Saturday, and half of Sunday in a classroom in Manhattan (conveniently located a few blocks from NYU—just in case) where using your native language is strictly forbidden.

I had entered the class on Friday evening with trepidation, still haunted by my classroom experience with Madame D—— forty years ago, not to mention my more recent brush with her online progeny, Mademoiselle D——. Sixteen hours trapped in a room with only three other students and an instructor: this is the type of thing that a poor teacher or one difficult student can make or break. When I see Marc, *le professeur,* though, I relax.

He's clearly French, possessing the kind of skinny you hardly ever see on American men anymore, and dressed in tight jeans, a narrow tie loosed at the neck, and unlaced work boots. His scarf has been draped over a chair in the front row, and his tightly cropped hair and beard are the same length, giving him a certain *je ne sais quoi.* In short, he is perfect, authentic, hip, and most of all very, very French. I am definitely going to learn some *français* this weekend.

"*Bonsoir,*" he begins. After handing out materials, he introduces himself, speaking slowly and deliberately, the way you'd speak to an infant, so that we can follow him (let's face it: if he spoke in a normal tempo, we'd all be lost). He says he was born in Rome. Cool! A true Continental man—how glamorous! He does look a little Italian, come to think of it. I'm liking this *homme* more and more. Born in Rome, most likely raised in Fran— "Rome, New York," he continues, interrupting my thoughts. What? That *un*glamorous former factory town in Upstate New York?

I'm amazed; this guy is more French than de Gaulle! How does he pull it off? Marc explains that after college he lived in France for several years and that he still returns frequently. I'm guessing *very* frequently. Consider this: One of the students is from Philadelphia, and Marc has to ask whether it's spelled *Phile-* or *Phila-,* precisely the kind of confusion that might be exhibited by a Frenchman. Later in the weekend, he struggles to come up with the English word for—he pantomimes because, remember, no English is allowed here—that leather thing you wear on your hip to hold a gun. "Holster?" I offer, almost enviously. *I* want to be Marc, to be mistaken for a Frenchman, to think, eat, be skinny, and most of all speak like a Frenchman.

Marc has each of us introduce ourselves and explain why we're here. Two middle-aged students are brushing up before vacations. A high school senior, heir apparent to a renowned local wine store, is preparing to spend the summer apprenticing at a vineyard in Burgundy. I'm the last to speak, and as I'm the only one in the room not already holding a ticket to Paris, I simply say, "*Je veux parler français.*" I want to speak French.

"*C'est tout?*"

No, that isn't all. I say in bad French—for I *have* picked up some French in the past nine months—that I want to spend summers in France, to go to French plays, watch French movies, read French newspapers. Maybe even retire to France, sitting in cafés and listening to the local gossip. I want to understand the menus, bargain with the vendors at the Paris flea market. And that's not all. My imagination now running faster than my French, I stammer that I want to play *pétanque,* I want to . . . to . . .

"*Surfer le Seine!*" Marc chimes in, with a Gallic wave of the hand.

"*Oui! Je veux surfer le Seine!*"

I don't know whether that's a French idiom or just Marc's colorful metaphor,* but it's a wonderful image I'll embrace as my own.

A student asks a question in English and is gently reprimanded as Marc explains, in slow, simple French, why we won't be speaking any English in class. French is not a translation of English, he says. It is not English that has been coded into French and needs to be back-coded into English to be understood. French is French. When French people say something in

---

* It's the latter.

French, it is not that they really mean something in English; no, they mean something in French. You cannot simply replace a French word with an English word. To understand what a French word means, you have to understand *les circonstances* in which it is used.

Take the simplest of French words, *bonjour.* Now, virtually every French course or textbook in the world will tell you that *bonjour* means "hello" and leave it at that, but Marc, using us as props, convincingly and with great agility demonstrates how it is not quite "hello," "hi," "good morning," "good day," nor "ahem, I'm here," although it can be any of those things. Well, what is it? *It's something French people say when they meet someone,* and instead of searching for the English equivalent, you should observe how it's used to understand its meaning.

When I want to say something in French, I think of what I want to say in English and then convert that into French. But such translation, I'd previously been told by David Birdsong, is self-limiting. You must remove the mental middleman of translation, for your brain cannot translate back and forth fast enough to keep up with a conversation. To achieve fluency, you need to speak—and think—like a bilingual, to switch languages, not translate between them. When you see a bird, you must think *oiseau,* not "bird . . . in French that's *oiseau.*" Of course, easier said than done.

Marc's French is superb and also quite different at times from the French I've been learning, far more colloquial. A number of times during the weekend—for example, when I ask a question using the textbook method of reversing the noun and verb to turn a statement ("You have a pen") into a question (*Avez-vous un stylo?*)—Marc tells me it's perfectly correct French . . . but very formal. Nobody in France speaks that way in casual conversation, he says. Instead, simply voice the statement with a rising inflection that implies a question: *Vous avez un stylo?*

Class moves quickly, and I try to stay with it and not worry about absorbing every little detail, but one particular idiosyncracy brings me, and by extension the class, to a dead stop. Marc writes the following phrase on the board: *Plus de gâteau!*

"How do we say this?" he asks in French. More cake? Come on, this is easy even for the beginner class down the hall. Anyone with a casual familiarity with French knows that the final consonant of a word is generally silent (except when the next word begins with a vowel). I read the phrase aloud, pronouncing *plus* with a silent *s,* so that the word sounds like "ploo," rhyming with "clue."

Correct? Well, Marc explains in French, with some terrific body language, that it depends on the situation. If I'm in a restaurant and, like many others that evening, I've ordered a slice of cake, the waiter might run into the kitchen and cry, "*Plus de gâteau!*" to the chef, pronouncing the *s* in *plus,* so that it sounds like "ploose." But if there is no more cake—the cake is gone, finished, kaput—the chef may respond, "*Plus de gâteau!*" Silent *s.*

"*Un moment,*" I interrupt. "Ploose" *de gâteau* means more cake, but "ploo" *de gâteau* means there's *no* more cake? Whether or not you pronounce the *s* reverses the meaning? It reminds me a bit of the word *personne,* which can mean either "person" or "*no* person (no one)," depending on the context.

"*Exactement!*" he exclaims.

This is *exactement* why French is such a pain in the *derrière.*

Given enough time, Marc says, you'll pick up the nuances.

And it's mastering the nuances that make you sound really French. Of course, the odds of my ever sounding really French are pretty close to zero. My pronunciation, Marc tells me kindly, is atrocious. Apparently I have a particular problem with the nasal sounds. French pronunciation relies far more on the nose than English does. The French use the nose almost as a musical instrument. Perhaps this is why satirical drawings of Frenchmen (even by Frenchmen) often feature an exaggerated nose.

A 1958 political caricature of Charles de Gaulle sporting a larger-than-life proboscis (and his actual nose was large enough to begin with) caused enough of an uproar in France to be noted in *Time* magazine. There are several distinct nasal phonemes in French that come from expelling air through the nose rather than through the mouth. You can experience three of them, giving your sinuses quite a workout, simply by ordering "a good white wine": *un bon vin blanc.*

Whenever things get dull, Marc throws up a short, humorous

video in French that we discuss as best we can, but the most memorable clip is from the American TV series *Reno 911!*, that hilarious spoof of the police reality show *Cops*. Season 1, episode 7, opens with Deputy Trudy Wiegel listening to a French instructional tape, the classic kind of language-phrase tape that used to be popular, in her squad car.

"We have two cats. *Nous avons deux chats.*"

And Wiegel repeats, "We have two cats."

"Everybody loves ham. *Tout le monde aime le jambon.*"

Wiegel repeats, with feeling: "*Every*body loves *ha-am*!"

And so on, and it's not until about the third phrase that you realize she's repeating the English, not the French. Wiegel is subsequently lulled to sleep by the tape (who hasn't been there?) and is discovered in her garage with both the tape and the engine still running, which results in her being put on a suicide watch, much to her bewilderment.

Suicide may be lurking in all our minds by the time immersion weekend is over. I stumble out of the elevator for the final time and meet Anne, who'd been wandering through museums while I was locked up with French, for lunch at a French restaurant.

I do wonder how much of this intensive French will stick. Short term, there's no problem. After seating us, the waiter (who is not French) asks if we need anything else. "*Non, merci,*" I reply reflexively. Anne is tickled, thinking that I've arrived, I'm speaking French—mission accomplished. *Moi,* I know I missed that *non* by a nose hair.

I miss the next French word by a mile. The restaurant has a selection of cocktails, all in French. *Côté voiture,* I see on the menu. What the heck is that? I know that I should know, because *voiture* is "car," and I've been drilled endlessly on *côté.* I remember *côté* is usually preceded by *à,* as in *à côté,* but for the life of me I can't remember the meaning.

"*Something* car," I say aloud. "*Something* car." But what?

Meanwhile, Anne has abandoned the French and is reading the description: "Cognac, Grand Marnier . . . it's a sidecar." Anne may not speak French, but she does know her mixology.*

Over drinks, she casually mentions, "I had a patient with an accent problem last week."

"Really?" I say, only half listening, still smarting over the sidecar incident.

"She had a small stroke and now speaks with a German accent."

"Uh-huh." It's a fine sidecar, with sugar on the rim.

"She's not German, has no German relatives, and has never been to Germany."

I almost drive my *côté voiture* off the road. "Foreign accent syndrome! Do you have any idea how rare that is?" Anne has had an incredibly unlikely encounter with FAS, a mere hundred

---

* You may, however, commit a faux pas if you order a *côté voiture* in France, where the drink, which may well have originated in Paris, is nevertheless more likely to be called (Académie française members, brace yourselves) *un side-car.*

cases of which have ever been reported in the literature. The first widely reported instance involved a Norwegian woman whose head was struck with shrapnel during a German air raid in 1941. As bad luck would have it, she emerged from the incident with not just *any* foreign accent but a strong *German* accent, which led to her being shunned by her village.

Most cases of FAS are attributed to a mild stroke rather than trauma, but in some cases the cause remains a mystery. In 2011 an American woman woke up from dental surgery with an Irish accent. FAS cases have included language changes from Japanese to Korean, British English to French, American English to British English, and even Spanish to Hungarian. One American woman, born and bred in Indiana, developed such a distinctive British accent after a stroke that it was identified by linguists as a mixture of English Cockney and West Country. Now, she might have seen *My Fair Lady* a few too many times, but surely she wouldn't know a West Country accent if she woke up with one. And the same was true not only for Anne's patient but for most FAS victims, who have not had significant exposure to the accents they were adopting. How, Professor 'iggins, do you explain this?

Researchers at Oxford University have concluded that what others hear as a foreign accent is actually a speech impediment that is mistakenly interpreted as an accent. For example, a patient with FAS might find that her attempt to pronounce the sound "is" comes out as "eez." It is also common for patients who have suffered trauma or mild stroke to put an even stress on every syllable, which is very unlike an English speaker (but very *like* a French speaker). Put the two together and you could conceivably get an accent that sounds a bit Pepé Le Pew.

Anne's patient most likely lost the ability to pronounce the letter *w*, which came out like a *v*. As for the changes in cadence, some scientists have suggested that once patients realize they're sounding foreign, it's easier to switch than to fight, so they adopt—subconsciously or otherwise—the language's cadence. In fact, some go a step further and start to adopt the mannerisms (or at least the perceived mannerisms, often exaggerated) of their "new" culture, becoming real-life Zeligs.

"Is she seeking treatment?" I ask Anne.

"There is no treatment."

"I see."

Anne must notice my brow furrowing in thought. "What is it?"

"I was just wondering . . . is her German better than my French?"

Fruit Flies When You're Having Fun
· ·

"What's that fish doing in my ear?"
"It's a Babel fish. It's translating for you."
—DOUGLAS ADAMS, *The Hitchhiker's Guide to the Galaxy*, 1979

Tell me if you've heard this one: God, according to the book of Genesis, which religious scholars date to the fifth or sixth century BC, is feeling a tad insecure because the city of Babel is erecting a skyscraper, taller than anything ever seen round those parts. The tower is rising alarmingly close to heaven, so close that the workers are only a few floors short of knocking on heaven's gate. Really, the last thing God needs is to have his minions construct a stairway to heaven. You have to *earn* your way there.

Something has to be done, but what? Now, this is where a lot of people get the story wrong: God does not destroy the Tower of Babel; He merely halts further construction, like a powerful union boss. Now, He could've opted to do this in any number of ways. This is, after all, God, the same God who stopped the sun dead in its tracks for twenty-four hours so the Israelites could finish off the Amorites at Gibeon. But God recognizes that the tower isn't so much the problem as the *symptom* of a problem.

The real issue is that the peoples of the world "have one language, and nothing will be withholden from them which they purpose to do." The gift of language is so mighty it poses a threat to God! So He famously says, "Come, let us go down and confound their speech."

Hang on a second. "Us?" Who's the "us"? Either God has company up there or He is using the royal "we," which, you'll remember, is descended from the Latin usage of *vos/nos* and led to the French power semantic, the *vous/tu* distinction.

In any event, He does (or they do) a thoroughly good and lasting job of confounding language. Unable to communicate, the workers abandon tower and city alike and go back to their previous business of waging war against one another, and to this day the world's been grappling with the problems of the planet's confounded tongues. Undoubtedly we haven't been nearly as close to heaven since.

Linguists and sadistic high school French teachers are not the only ones who have tried to deal with God's handiwork at Babel. Scientists have also taken a crack at this, and it's about time. Society, by which I mean the entertainment in-dustry, by which I mean science fiction movies and television, by which I probably mean *Star Trek,* has been dangling the promise of a computerized, universal translation device for four decades—most of my life. I honestly expected that by now I'd be wearing a Bluetooth-earpiece type of device that would translate spoken French into English and vice versa, and that would be that. I could travel anywhere in the world, from France to China to Boston, and understand and be understood without hundreds or thousands of hours of study.

More knowledgeable people than I have shared the same expectation. As recently as 2006, IBM included in its annual "5 in 5" list—five technologies they expect to see within five years—the prediction that 80 percent of the world's population would own mobile devices "capable of precise language trans-lation." They envisioned "a technology equivalent to Star Trek's universal translator—allowing two people speaking different languages to understand each other fluidly."

Wow. It's as if they were reading my mind, not to mention watching the same TV shows. But the company known as Big Blue didn't make the prediction out of the blue; IBM was al-ready working on such a device. And you'd think that if any-one could pull off this technological feat, it would be IBM, the company that built Watson, the computer that absolutely creamed the two greatest *Jeopardy!* champions the world has ever known.

Well, the five years are up, and my French is down, so instead of spending another morning trying to remember that in the upside-down world of French a literal "young girl" (*jeune fille*) is older than a "girl" (*fille*), I've come to visit Watson and his colleagues at the IBM Thomas J. Watson Research Center, not far from my home in the Hudson Valley, to see firsthand how far IBM has come toward realizing their prediction of an earpiece of Babel—and whether the technology might soon bail me and my French out.

Watson, massive and silent behind a glass wall in a darkened room like a high-tech Buddha, is resting, but Bowen Zhou, the manager of the speech-to-speech translation project at the Watson labs, is here to greet me. IBM has been working on computerized language translation for decades, for not only is communication important to this prototypical global company—after all, the *I* in IBM stands for "International"—there is potentially big prestige and bigger money to be won here. The European Union alone spends a billion euros a year on human translators.

Since well before Watson's day, decades before there was such a thing as Google, computer scientists have been working on this problem. The origin of machine translation virtually coincides with the invention of the digital computer. The first published paper on the subject appears in 1949. It was almost as if scientists said, "Okay, we have this thing we're calling a computer. What the heck are we going to do with it?" and someone piped up, "I'm going to Italy next year and don't speak a word. How about we get it to translate?"

Why not? This would seem to be the type of thing computers excel at, but in reality it turns out to be a deceptively difficult task, one that defeated the best and brightest minds of two generations. Before a computer can translate between two languages, it first has to "learn" each of them. This means programming each language, its syntax and lexicon and rules, into the computer and then constructing a mapping between the languages.

Even while computers were flying airplanes and defeating chess grand masters (the checkmating computer known as Deep Blue is an IBM machine as well), computerized language translation continued to thwart scientists for all the reasons that French has been thwarting me: language is recursive ("John went to the store in the middle of the town that he moved to last year"); language is full of exceptions ("*la nouvelle cuisine*"; "*la cuisine chaude*"); language is ambiguous ("John threw Paul the ball"; "John threw up").

Consider the two nearly identical sentences "The pen is in the box" and "The box is in the pen." The words for a writing instrument and an enclosure for animals happen to be the same in English, but that is unlikely to be the case in any other language; thus the machine needs to possess knowledge of the sizes of things in the physical world before it can supply a correct translation. Not surprisingly, early efforts at machine translation produced as many howlers as they did accurate, or even understandable, translations.

Feeling that there had to be a better way, in 1990 Peter Brown and three colleagues at the Watson Research Center published a groundbreaking paper that would fundamentally change the way that scientists approach computerized language translation. Brown argued that we should forget trying to teach the rules and syntax of language to a computer; that's a fool's errand. His approach didn't rely on any knowledge of language at all. Rather, he proposed a statistical, data-driven model, in which the computer would have at its disposal a large database that recorded how professional translators—that is, real human beings—had previously translated words, phrases, and sentences from one language into another, and then the computer would search this database to find the most statistically probable match to the phrase being translated.

Take the phrase "good morning." The computer searches its database and finds that "good morning" appears one hundred times. Eighty-two times it has been translated (by humans) as *bonjour;* twelve times, as *bon matin;* and six times, as *bonne matinée.* The computer chooses *bonjour* as the most likely translation.

Most likely, but not always correct. If the full sentence is "Good morning, sir," the translation *bonjour* is correct, but if the context is, "You know it's going to be a good morning when the newspaper lands near the door," the statistically improbable *bon matin* is correct. If the speaker is leaving the *boulangerie* and wants to wish the clerk a good remainder of the morning, the even less statistically likely *bonne matinée* is the right translation.

Some of this information can be inferred from the phrase's placement in the sentence, so you must have your software parse out and match the word, phrase, and sentence alignments (something called parameter estimation) and know something about the order of phrases in both the source and the target languages to get it right. As IBM's Bowen Zhou explains to me, "You learn the word alignments first, then you extract patterns. We are trying to understand the hierarchical structure of languages. You cannot treat a language as just a string of words."

In other words, it's not merely a game of probabilities. Still, this statistical model of language translation that Brown was suggesting in 1990 was a totally novel approach, a far cry from trying to teach a computer the syntax and conjugations of a language. It was so radical that, backed by Brown's promising early results, it startled, then changed, the field of machine translation.

When you think about it, the approach makes sense. It's not dissimilar to the way a child learns a first language. He hears all this noise around him and may hear words in different contexts, with different representations, but over time he learns which meanings are the most likely for these new sounds. He also hears a lot of incorrect and fragmentary language and is able to filter out the good from the bad, partly because the good outnumbers—is more statistically probable than—the bad. The toddler's database is the world of voices around him. But what's the database for a computer? Where do you find enough quality translations between two languages for even a pilot project?

Canada. By law, all the proceedings of the Canadian Parliament must be recorded in both English and French. By 1990, all these transcripts, known as the Hansard, were available in computer-readable format, some hundred million words that Brown was able to obtain from the Canadian government. From that treasure trove his team was able to extract three million matching English-French sentence pairs, a modern-day Rosetta Stone.

Of course, in their test translations they didn't always or even usually find an exact match for the input sentence (remember my earlier statement that it is likely that every sentence on this page has never appeared in print before). When they didn't find a sentence match (which was about 95 percent of the time), they would drop down to the next level, trying to match a cluster of words in the sentence. If they found a cluster match, they would save it and move on to the next cluster. Once all the clusters were resolved, it was time to do the hardest part: construct a grammatically correct sentence in French from these French clusters.

When the computer doesn't find a match for even a cluster of words, it seeks a match for each single word in the cluster. Here's where things get really hazardous. For example, if you want to translate the word "hear" into French, you're probably going to be using some form of the verb *entendre*. Yet in Brown's early tests, the computer bizarrely translated "hear" into *bravo* every time, because when searching the database for "hear," forms of *entendre* came up less than 1 percent of the time. The other 99 percent of the time "hear" was translated as *bravo*.

What gives? Well, in the Canadian Parliament, when a speaker says something members approve of, they respond with shouts— dutifully recorded by the stenographer—of "Hear, hear!" while the Québécois delegates shout "Bravo!" so in this context the translation is quite correct. But it skews the database, ludicrously translating "I hear you" into *je vous bravo,* one of those howlers I referred to earlier. Well, how do you get around this? By telling the computer that one "hear" means *entendre* and two of them back-to-back mean *bravo.*

Another way you get around this problem is by increasing the size of your database, drawing from a wider body and variety of translations. And by the middle of the next decade, the Internet would make that not only possible but relatively easy. And who is better at scouring the Internet for data than Google? Building on IBM's research on the statistical model of language translation, Google ditched their old rules-based program in 2006, launching their own statistically based product,

Google Translate, which soon became the most popular translation engine in the world, displacing such early entries as BabelFish.

What websites does Google visit to get reliable translations? "All official United Nations documents are required to be published in the six official UN languages," Jeff Chin, lead product manager for Google Translate, told me over the phone. As are all documents of the European Union, which has twenty-three official languages. It turns out that there are a surprising number of translated documents on the Web, from online books to political reports to newspapers to blogs, and the first thing that statistical translation software does is "document alignment," identifying which documents are translations of others, filtering out spam, deliberately malicious translations, and the like before proceeding with sentence, phrase, and then word alignment.

The explosion of the Web has allowed Google to include to date 80 languages that can be translated into any of the others, offering 6,320 potential language pairs. Of course, the pairs with the greatest number of available translated documents are going to produce the most accurate matches, so English-Spanish translations tend to be more reliable than, say, Vietnamese-Yiddish. In fact, there may be almost no Vietnamese works translated into or from Yiddish, but there *are* English works, from novels to news stories, that have been translated into both Vietnamese and Yiddish, and those two corresponding documents can be aligned.

The chief limitation with the Google approach is that it is all done on their server farms, requiring an Internet connection. IBM has taken a different approach. "We envision that speech translation is something that you carry with you all the time," Bowen Zhou says to me as we sit in his IBM lab. "Think of where you are when you're doing speech translation. You are often in a foreign country, far away from home, maybe in the middle of nowhere. You may have no Internet connection, or if you do, it may be expensive. He pulls an off-the-shelf smartphone out of his pocket and places it in airplane mode, disabling its cellular and wi-fi connections. "This is my everyday phone," the Chinese-born Zhou says, "with our program loaded on it." Then he presses the volume-up button and says something in Chinese. A moment later I hear a natural-sounding male voice say, "I enjoyed my stay in Tokyo and I *really* like this meeting," putting emphasis on "really," while the words appear on the screen.

Zhou hands me the phone, and I ask for a coffee, which he confirms is correctly translated into Chinese, and then he says something in Chinese in return, and we have a brief conversation, not perfect, but not bad, with the smartphone as intermediary. Although I never do get the coffee.

The speech recognition is impressive as well and improves with use as it learns your voice. Harkening back to my days as a computer programmer, I wonder aloud, "How on earth did you squeeze all of this onto a smartphone?"

"It comes with a compromise," Zhou says, explaining that they have intentionally limited the vocabulary and scope in order to do a limited thing well, instead of trying to do everything for everyone. The software, which was first deployed in Iraq under a Defense Department contract, is strong on military and infrastructure language, but weak on, say, sports.

Zhou encourages me to challenge the device, so I say, "Time flies when you're having fun." This isn't quite as cheeky as it may seem; I chose the phrase "time flies" because, surprisingly, my French pen pal, Sylvie, with her limited command of English, had used it in a recent note. The software recognizes my English correctly but doesn't know the idiom. Zhou says the Chinese it returned is too literal a translation, as if time had wings, but is otherwise correct and understandable to a Chinese speaker. Undeterred, I give it the acid test. "Fruit flies like spoiled peaches." He shakes his head. It translated it as fruit flying through the air. Apparently it hasn't been trained in entomology, either.

For comparison, I later speak both sentences into Google Translate on my smartphone. It also has trouble with fruit flies, spitting back something about fruit flies being like peaches that have been spoiled (as in, treated too well).

But my fruit-fly example was a trick question, and I feel a little bad. Almost forgetting I'm talking to a device, I sympathetically say to Zhou's phone, "Learning a language is hard," unintentionally throwing another curveball, as it interprets "hard" not as "difficult" but as the opposite of soft.

"If you look at where we are today," Zhou says, "machine translation is a glass with half water," inadvertently illustrating one of the challenges of machine translation and the twenty-five thousand English idioms to be learned. "In only twenty years, we've come a long ways." Just how do they fill up that glass of water? "The key here is using context," Zhou says, "looking at words beyond the sentence boundaries"—to know, for example, whether the sentence before "language is hard" was "Gypsum is soft" or "I'm studying French."

Another tack IBM is taking with translation goes in a different direction entirely. They want to make the computer more interactive, to introduce a dialogue assistant (will they call it HAL?) that will say, "I don't understand which sense of 'hard' you intend. Please explain." Zhou sees the computer as a third, interactive party in the translation process.

I ask Zhou, as I did earlier with Jeff Chin at Google, how many years we are from the kind of machine speech-to-speech translation that realizes the science fiction dream, that will allow people like me to live in Paris or Prague without years of study, followed perhaps by days of embarrassment and misunderstanding. Unsurprisingly, neither will commit, but I recently learned about a demonstration at Georgetown University in which Russian was machine-translated into English.

The results were so remarkable that front-page coverage in the *New York Times* and other prominent newspapers and magazines included predictions from linguists that within five years the problem of machine language translation would be solved.

The date of the *Times* article was January 8, 1954. I was nine months old.

Bah, Ouais!

. . . .

It's great you can come here soon bill, me and my
fiancé will be very happy to meet you in Paris :) I thought
if it is possible to go for a walk in Paris, or doing shopping
together :) if you want or what would you like to do
in Paris? there is a lot of possibilities down there.
—E-mail from Sylvie

Katie and I are both packing for trips, and it's hard to tell who's
more stressed out. "I'm going to Ghana in a week and I don't
speak a word of Twi!" she says.

"Yeah, well, I'm going to France in two weeks and I barely
speak any French."

"That's not true, Dad. You've learned a lot of French since
the last time I was home. Besides, you're going to France to

study French. And if you think French is hard, you ought to try Twi."

Katie is preparing for a semester abroad in Ghana. Although English is the official language, Twi is the country's most widely spoken language, and since Katie will be living with a family near Accra while attending classes at the university, she feels it's the polite thing to be able to speak to her hosts (and others) in their vernacular language.

"It's a tonal language."

"What does that mean?"

She demonstrates, her voice rising up and down like she's singing. "There are three tones, high, low, and medium, which are part of the pronunciation. A word that has one meaning in a low tone might have an entirely different meaning when said in a high tone." She sings again.

That *does* sound harder than French.

"What's your name in Twi?" I ask.

Katie looks at me like I'm crazy and makes a face. "Ummm, Katie?"

"*Moi, je suis Guy.*"

"*Bonjour, Papa Guy.*"

The name had been bestowed upon me a few days earlier at the latest gathering of my French Meetup group, this one at a member's house in celebration of the group's two-year anniversary. It was a pleasant but staid affair. Staid, that is, until Pierre, an advanced speaker whom I'd never met, strode in, filling the room with his *joie de vivre*. A large man with tousled hair who tossed down *vin rouge* at a Gallic pace, he looked at my name tag, which read "Bill," and said, "*Ah, Guillaume!*" the French version of "William."

But Guillaume was too formal for him. "*Quel est le* 'nick-name' *pour Guillaume?*" he'd asked the room.

"Guy," someone offered. Of course! As in Guy de Maupassant (pronounced "ghee"). As Pierre refilled both my wineglass and his, he'd told me, in French (this was an immersion party, of course), that I was in fact not Bill, but Guy. I needed to *be* French if I was going to *learn* French. "I'm a musician, a natural performer," he said. "It's easy for me. But you can do it, too." His words echoed the advice of Catherine, my French Skype pal, who'd lectured me on the *plaisir* of being French. I thought also of Marc, the New School immersion teacher who put this theory into practice so convincingly I was sure he was French.

A few days later, with Katie fretting over Twi, and me over French, I have a chance to trot out Guy when Katie's college roommate Chloé, a French exchange student, stops by for a brief visit. "*Je m'appelle Guy,*" I say, shaking hands, before continuing with the typical French greeting.

"*Ça va?*"

"*Ça va. Ça va?*"

"*Ça va.*"

This may sound to the uninitiated like we're just repeating

the same two words over and over, like a stuck record, but in fact we've had quite the chat.

"How are you?"

"I'm fine. How are you?"

"Pretty well."

With a lexicon a third the size of ours, the French have learned to be efficient with language; thus you can *Ça va* your way quite far into a conversation knowing only two words of French, and two-letter words at that! The downside is that the French person to whom you're speaking can get lulled into a false sense of your fluency, as is the case with Chloé, who responds with something that sounds like *Merghiporxlhusxlahdograntionmcskeksé*.

This has the effect of peeling off my Guy mask, revealing William-who-doesn't-speak-French. William humbly asks for a translation.

"I love your kitchen. I feel like I am in France! The colors, the . . . how you say . . . copper pots, the pottery, *la musique. C'est très français.*"

Well, I got that part right, at least, even if I still can't pronounce *rouge*. Over dinner, I tell Chloé of my woes in learning French, figuring she'll be more sympathetic than Katie. Word stress is not distinctive in French, I point out; the syllables within individual words are pronounced with near-equal emphasis, making them more difficult to pick up. For example, in English we say "in-*tel*-li-gent," with a clear stress on the second syllable, a cue that helps the nonnative listener recognize the word. In French, it's pronounced "*ahn-tel-le-gent*," with a monotone pronunciation, giving near-equal emphasis to all four syllables before going on to the next monotone word, which may well be connected with a liaison. Generally, if any syllable is stressed, it's the final one, but even then only lightly.

Chloé is, of course, unaware of this. She's also baffled that I find the French numbering system difficult. "Eighty," I say, "is *quatre-vingts*—four twenties! It's multiplication!"

"But we don't think of it that way. It's just *quatre-vingts*, just a word you learn."

Oh.

I should've known better than to complain to a French-woman about the French language. "You want to talk about numbers," Chloé says in her charmingly accented English, becoming animated. "English is much worse. You have these strange . . . measurements! I never know what is zee temperature here! Why do you go from thirty-two to . . . what is it, two hundred twenty?"

"Two hundred twelve."

"For us, you see, water freezes at zey-ro and boils at one hundred. It's easy!" She slaps her hand on the table.

No argument there. But she's not done. "And I cannot cook here! Cups, ounces, pints, and tablespoons, and . . . what is zee other one?"

"Teaspoon."

"Teaspoon! What eez a teaspoon?"

"A third of a tablespoon," I say sheepishly, as if I'm somehow responsible.

Her eyes grow large. "A *third*! . . . How do you . . . you . . . remember all this . . . these . . . things?"

"Well, *you* must have to remember something."

"Milliliters."

Silence. That's all.

"How's the wine?" I ask, hoping she'll say it goes down like the baby Jesus in velvet underpants, but she just says, "Very nice."

"It's Californian."

"Your wine is not bad here."

"So you like America."

"*Bah, ouais!*" she responds, pronouncing *ouais*, roughly the French "yeah," as "way."

"*Bah, ouais? Qu'est-ce que c'est?*" I ask.

Katie jumps in. "It's sort of like a hipster version of 'Well, duh!' Baaaaah, way!"

Hipster French? I must try that out in France.

I had misinterpreted Chloé's distaste for the imperial measurement system as distaste for of America, but nothing could be further from the truth. "What do you like about America?"

"The people are more open, more friendly here. And there are more opportunities. I want to come back here to live after I finish school."

No way, I tell her. I can't wait to get to France, and she can't wait to get out!

"What do you like about France?" she asks.

I rhapsodize about the food, the physical beauty of the countryside, the quality of the light in Paris, the culture, especially the films, the fact that the French value their heritage and architecture, while we, in the name of progress, tear down gems like New York's old Pennsylvania Station.

She takes it all in, smiles, and replies slowly, so I can understand, "*L'herbe est toujours plus verte de l'autre côté.*"

She either said the grass is always greener on the other side or asked for a sidecar.

Botte Camp

··

He can speak French in Russian.
—Dos Equis commercial featuring the
Most Interesting Man in the World

I lean over and whisper, "*J'ai un petit problème,*" which, you
may remember from my Gallic bicycling adventure, is loosely
translated as, "I'm back in France." This time, *sans* Anne and
bicycle, for this trip is all business—the business of learning
French. After a year of escalating study, progressing from self-
study software and podcasts to social networking to a weekend
class, I've come for what I hope will be the *coup de grâce*—two
intense weeks at Millefeuille Provence, a total-immersion (*bain
linguistique,* or "linguistic bath") language school in southern
France.

Upon my arrival two days earlier, I'd proved that one can

in fact drown in a bath. I'd been met by a young man named Philippe, who'd given me my room keys, including a huge key of the old-fashioned kind that you'd more expect to find opening a cell at the Bastille than admitting you to a French-language school in Provence.

The bedroom and front door keys I'd understood, but when Philippe had tried to explain what this large one was for in slow, simple French, all I could do was apologetically say, "*Désolé, je ne comprends pas.*" Over and over. He'd tried a couple of different approaches and then finally said something that sounded like "eff-euh."

"*Eff-euh?*" I repeated. "*Qu'est-ce que c'est, eff-euh?*"

"*She-mee? Vous connaissez she-mee? Eff-euh.*"

She-mee, she-mee, she-mee. I had that word in Rosetta Stone, damn it! What was *she-mee*?

"*She-mee? Comme physique, mathématiques. Chimie.*"

Oh, chemistry! "*Ah, oui! Chimie!*"

"*Oui!*"

"*Oui.*"

All this *oui*-ing was *oui*-derful, but what in the name of Napoleon's ghost was the key for? The chemistry lab? Finally, out of desperation, he grabbed a scrap of paper and wrote down the mysterious "eff-euh."

The letters "Fe." The symbol for iron, as written in the periodic table of elements. The Frenchman who didn't speak English and the American who didn't speak French had found a universal language, the language of chemistry, to untwist our tied tongues. And more importantly for me, to unlock the iron gate to the school grounds. The gate, a heavy, Louis XVI–era model, had caught my attention on the way in, especially when it clanked shut—locked—behind me, making me jump. I didn't see a sign overhead that read, ABANDON ALL HOPE, YE WHO ENTER HERE, although the school's strict rule is "Abandon all languages but French, ye who enter here."

Millefeuille Provence accepts a maximum of eighteen students at any given time, to keep class sizes to no more than four, but I am lucky. This first week we are an intimate group of nine, and my classes will vary from two to three.

Over dinner I meet most of the other students, about half of whom, like me, have just arrived. The other half are about to begin their second and final week. The gang of nine includes James, an affable, young British financial consultant; a Czech banker and his wife, who are relocating to Paris for his job; a British energy consultant who has been living in Paris for three years; an Indian doctor working in disaster relief; and a Swedish woman whose name I'll never remember, and even if I could, I wouldn't be able to pronounce it, so I'll end up just calling her (but not to her face) Inger Stevens, after the sixties actress best known for the television series *The Farmer's Daughter*. This Inger is a classic Swede, a tall blond who, come September, will be Sweden's deputy ambassador to France.

These students are all learning French for business reasons.

The final two members of our group, coincidentally both from Manhattan, are here for pleasure. Karen is a sweet, street-smart retiree in her seventies; the other student, a BlackBerry-addicted, iPad-addled attorney whose job is looking after her husband's high-tech patents, which, I will learn, is a euphemism for suing everyone in sight. (Thus in the interest of staying out of court, I'll not give even her first name. Or her hair color.)

When my turn comes to introduce myself to the group, I say, "*Je m'appelle Guy,*" determined to live as my French alter ego for the next two weeks, to leave the timid, language-hesitant, self-conscious, all-American Bill behind, no matter how challenging that is.

My choice of Millefeuille was a careful one. There are scores of language schools in France, but the majority of them are geared toward language vacations: a few hours of class in the morning to feel virtuous, and then you hit the beach and the shops. Well, there is no beach within a hundred miles of this highly regarded school, which caters to governments, businesses, and NGOs, and fewer shops—in fact nothing to distract you from the work at hand. What the neighborhood does have is lots of grapes, with vineyards in every direction as far as the eye can see. Millefeuille, which shares its space with an active winery, is in the heart of the Côtes du Rhône appellation (which means we'll be drinking good wine with dinner every evening). I hang out in the garden with the other students for a bit, then retreat to my room in the eighteenth-century château, and am awakened in the middle of the night by a short arrhythmia. Unfortunately, Guy has come to France with Bill's heart, which, after two surgeries and a half million bucks, is still keeping worse time than the antique clock in the hallway.

I'm sure it's nothing, and I'd had a few of these at home, always while lying down, but I don't appreciate that my *cœur* feels it necessary to remind me that I'm four thousand miles away from Anne, home, and my other home—NYU Langone Medical Center. Anne would've preferred I skip this trip, but knew better than to try to dissuade me from something I'm determined to do. While I turned down her backup plan— accompanying me—as unnecessarily protective and expensive, I did gratefully accept her backup of her backup plan, the quickest itinerary from Provence to NYU, which I have tucked safely in my wallet, with phone numbers.

ON MONDAY MORNING, AFTER a typical French breakfast of croissants, bread, and yogurt, we new students undergo written and oral evaluations, after which the groups are made up for the coming week. I've done well on the written portion, but not surprisingly for someone who's learned a language mainly via self-study, my oral skills are weaker. At ten thirty everyone gathers in the salon for a coffee break. It's a break from class but not from French, for me a difficult half hour of trying to make small talk in French while scanning the front pages of *Le Monde* and *Le Figaro* for news of home. The only encouraging thing is that I'm far from the only one who cannot pronounce the name of the school; even the advanced students have trouble, making me wonder if "Millefeuille" (as in the pastry—it means "thousand sheets") was chosen for its humbling unpronounceability. Near the end of the half hour, the diversion of watching one of the instructors trying to pry this word from the mouths of Czechs, Swedes, Brits, and Americans comes to a sudden halt when someone cries, "*La liste est affichée!*" and the salon empties as quickly as if she'd yelled, "*Feu!*"

La liste is a color-coded chart with cards indicating each student's grouping and schedule for the coming week. As everyone else rushes over to see, I follow tentatively. This has a real déjà vu feeling, and not in a good way, and after the buzz subsides I casually wander over to the list, hoping I made varsity. I am paired with James and Alyana, the wife of the Czech banker.

During our first class together, we are required to speak a few words about ourselves, in French, it goes without saying, and I learn that James has a good reason for being here. His employer, a prominent British financial firm, has offered to send him to INSEAD, the prestigious business school in Fontainebleau, to get his MBA, all expenses paid plus a stipend to live on. But there's a catch: even though classes are taught in English, the entrance exam he must pass next week is in French. He has the highest stakes, yet remarkably, is the most relaxed and laid back of us all. "It's an easy exam," he says (all the conversation in this chapter, whether related in English or French, is spoken in French).

Perhaps, but in *French*! I almost blurt aloud.

Soon after, we break for lunch. Because Millefeuille is essentially in the middle of nowhere, all meals are provided during the week, the quality varying from the sublime (Provençal fish soup) to the, well, surprising (eggplant with turkey—yes, the French eat turkey after they tire of duck breast and foie gras). We are always joined by one of the instructors at lunch, as meals do double duty as yet more immersion.

Students dribble in, food appears, but no one lifts a fork until the instructor wishes us *bon appétit,* the French equivalent of saying grace. One thing I've noticed about the French: they are always wishing you a *bon* something. When you enter a shop you are greeted with *bonjour;* when you leave it, *bonne journée* (have a nice day). In the afternoon, you may be wished a *bon après-midi* or its more loquacious cousin, *passez un bon après-midi.* Late in the afternoon, come some magical time that only the French know, *bonjour* becomes *bonsoir* when you come and *bonne soirée* when you go. In between, at dinner, you may be wished *bon appétit* before you eat and *bonne continuation* during. At the end of the meal, the waiter might wish you a *bonne fin de repas* or even (and this one is a little too clinical for my taste) a *bonne fin de digestion.*

Then there's *bon courage.* This is often shortened to just

"*Courage!*" with which we're already familiar. I'm always a little thrown when I hear French people parting with this greeting, especially when it's directed at me. This is the most difficult one of these *bon* phrases to translate, for, depending on the situation, it can mean anything from "have a nice day no matter what may come" to an ominous "good luck," sometimes with a nuance of "good luck, pal—you're going to need it!" I suspect in my case it's usually the last, and I do need it. At the table I'm asked to introduce myself again.

"*Je m'appelle Bill,*" I say, greatly confusing the students to whom I'd previously introduced myself as Guy. But after the morning's classes I've realized that the teachers know me as "Bill," the binder they've handed me is labeled "Bill," no other students have taken a French name (because we're not—*bah, ouais!*—in junior high school), and I feel silly about the whole Guy thing. It's going to be a grueling two weeks, and Guy's not going to be able to get me out of this fix by swinging down from a chandelier with a sword in one hand and a glass of *vin rouge* in the other, so I dismiss him.

In some ways these casual lunchtime and coffee-break encounters with the other students are more difficult than the classes, because we all speak French at different levels. Plus, the Slavs speak French with a Slavic accent, the Germans with a German accent, and so on. If you think it's difficult to understand French, try understanding French spoken with a strong Slavic accent. Only Inger speaks what sounds to me like polished French. In fact, her French is so good I wonder why she's here. (I'm told later that her ambassadorial position in Paris requires that her French be more than "so good.")

There are five instructors at the school, all skilled, up to the challenges of teaching a foreign language *in that language.* This demands that you be a bit of an actor as well as a teacher, and the instructors can be quite entertaining as they mime words. But the material and the schedule are demanding. Feeling as though it must be near the end of the day, I sneak a peek at my watch to see that it's only three o'clock, meaning that I still have *two* more classes to go.

When five thirty finally arrives, I'm a basket case. Fortunately, the school has a beautiful pool, so I grab my goggles and start swimming with a vengeance, trying to clear my head, needing to wash away the stress of my first day of language boot camp. Other students come and go until after lap *soixante-dix* I peek my head above water to see that I'm alone, save for one of the instructors, who'd been backstroking alongside my crawl. As she rinses off under the poolside shower, I remove my goggles, quickly check my pulse, and then attempt to compliment her on her lovely backstroke.

"*Vous avez une belle . . .*" Uh, I don't know the word, so I mime a backstroke.

She completes the sentence: *derrière* something?

Oh, my goodness, no! I wasn't admiring your buttocks!

She must see the panic in my eyes, for she repeats the words more slowly, though I never do really get them. Then she makes some swimmer's small talk. One thing I have to say about Millefeuille: Every interaction with a student is viewed as a teaching moment. Even when you pass the chambermaid in the hallway, she doesn't just say *bonjour,* she stops what she's doing to converse with you: Where are you from? Are you staying here for the weekend? It clearly is part of their job, and a nice touch.

On the subject of chambermaids, back in New York a hotel chambermaid has accused one Dominique Strauss-Kahn, head of the International Monetary Fund and presumed next president of France, of rape. Strauss-Kahn, who claims the sex was consensual, missed escaping the long arm of American law—it does not extend as far as France, which has no extradition treaty with the United States—by only a few minutes, having been hauled off a plane as it sat on the tarmac at JFK.

France is abuzz over *l'affaire DSK* and the indelicate handling of Strauss-Kahn by the New York courts, who have slapped this man of privilege and wealth into a cell on Rikers Island. This front-page news allows our resident lawyer, given her extensive experience with the American court system, to relish the role of expert witness, while providing the rest of us, teachers and students alike, with something to talk about during breaks. The something, however, will turn out to be the virtues of *Saint DSK* (whose rape charge has *elevated* his standing in France) and the unfairness of the American judicial system.

This evening's guest—there's one every night—gives a lecture, in rapid French, on French politics. I understand barely a word. Then dinner, which is served precisely at eight. These are leisurely ninety-minute or longer soirées, consisting of an appetizer and talk, a main course and talk, a cheese course accompanied by more talk, dessert served up with a side of talk, and finally café klatch in the garden, an opportunity for *serious* talk. At ten o'clock, a full thirteen hours after the first class began, I excuse myself to go to my room—to do my homework for tomorrow.

When the alarm wakes me on Tuesday morning, I can hardly drag myself out of bed. I'll be okay once I get going, but right now a full day of French immersion holds all the appeal of going to the dentist. Little do I know that I won't have to choose between the two. During lunch, speaking French goes from the theoretical to the practical, from hobby to necessity, when, biting into a salad with lettuce and olives (and at least one olive pit), I feel and hear a sickening crunch in my mouth. My tongue explores the bottom right-hand corner of my mouth to discover a crater the size of Marseilles where a filling used to be. I'm not even sure all the tooth is still there.

This, of course, is the *petit problème* I referred to earlier. I tell the instructor at the table, "*J'ai cassé une dent.*" She looks concerned for only an instant, before cheerily telling me it's not a crisis at all but an opportunity to put my French to work—to make an appointment, discuss the problem with the dentist, and so on. Good Lord, I'm not ready! Couldn't they have waited till the end of next week to toss olive pits into the salad?

It turns out she's half joking, and her assistance in fact goes much further than showing me to a telephone. The director will call a dentist and get me an appointment, but she can't call before two o'clock, because the dentist's office is closed for lunch between noon and two. In cities this custom is changing, but in rural France, it seems that most French workers still go home for an extended lunch, shuttering up their shops and offices. After my own aborted lunch I go for a walk and get an inkling of what some of them do with that time when, passing a house in the tiny village near the school, I hear the unmistakable cries of a woman in the throes of passion. She's definitely having a better lunch than I am, I think, as I return to school.

The director meets me inside the gate. I have a dental appointment at three. It takes a few passes for me to understand the arrangements, but I finally figure out that the cook will take me there and back. At the dentist's office, we pass through a door marked SALLE D'ATTENTE. Inside it's indistinguishable from a typical American waiting room, lined with chairs and magazines, but with one big difference. There are no other people here, not even a receptionist. Don't we need to check in with someone? Fill out some paperwork and sign some privacy forms? I wonder how the receptionist even knows we're here.

Turns out, there *is* no receptionist. At 3:03 the dentist herself, a woman of about sixty, comes in and escorts me into a spacious, modern examination room. Just one room, with a tiny adjoining office. No receptionists, no billers, no office managers, no dental technicians, no half-dozen cramped exam rooms that the dentist races between while you wait forever with an uncomfortable clamp in your mouth so that he never wastes a single income-producing moment. Just this one, sunny, expansive room with a dentist's chair.

Peering into my mouth, she pronounces, "*Ce n'est pas grave.*" Whew! Just a lost filling, which she replaces in ten minutes, but the tooth is fragile, she warns me, and I may need a *couronne* when I return home.

A what?

"*Une couronne.*"

I still don't understand. She mimes a crown on her head.

"*Comme un roi!*" I exclaim, feeling like I've just won at charades.

I always get excited when a word that means two different things in English means the same two things in French. Like hairpin curve, for example. You wouldn't necessarily expect that the French would also use the analogy of a hairpin to describe a sharp bend in the road, but in fact they do, calling it an *épingle à cheveux,* a word-for-word translation. My favorite, though, is "honeymoon," *lune de miel,* literally "moon of honey." Of course, you have to be careful in assuming a common English term can be translated similarly into French. You'll get puzzled glances if you tell the waiter there's too much of a foamy *tête* atop your glass of beer. If you are drowning and need a life jacket thrown to you, don't ask for *une veste de vie.* They'll have no idea what you're talking about and will probably have collapsed in laughter while you go under. What you need, I learned on my flight over, is *un gilet de sauvetage,* or a rescue vest, which actually makes more sense than "life jacket."

The dentist's bill, which I pay in cash, is forty euros, about fifty-seven dollars. All in all, my brush with the French health care system has been an entirely positive, not to mention educational, experience. Married to a doctor, I may be biased, but I find the notion of a medical professional who doesn't need any staff and can come home for two hours every afternoon for lunch and sex quite sensible.

Forty-five minutes after leaving the school—less than three hours after my mishap—I am back at Millefeuille, happy to be going home with a little souvenir of France in my mouth.

"*Je suis fini,*" I announce to my class.

Cécile looks horrified. "*Vous êtes fini? Non! Désolée!*"

What did I say wrong? Cécile flops her head and lets her tongue fall slack to demonstrate that *je suis fini* means "I'm dead." *J'ai fini* means "I've finished." I wonder if I will ever learn this language.

After class I stop in to thank the director, and when I comment on the efficiency of the French health care system, she pulls what looks like a credit card from her wallet. It's her health insurance card. Pointing to its embedded chip—you can see the little wires coming out of it—she tells me it contains her entire medical record: history, medications, and allergies. All physicians and hospitals have the equipment to read the card on a computer, to display and to update all the information. Thus not only does every doctor in France have access to your medical record, but should you be found unconscious and taken to an emergency room, no problem: they read your card and have your entire medical history in front of them.

So while American politicians continue to argue about universal health care, and doctors are just beginning the painful transition to dozens of different privatized electronic medical record (EMR) systems, none of which will talk to any of the others, and not one of which will give you one corpuscle of benefit should you be found unconscious somewhere, France already has a universal EMR on a chip that you carry with you.

What a wonderful country! If only they would discover the shower curtain, so I wouldn't have to bathe by sitting in a bathtub filled with two inches of water while maneuvering a handheld spray head, which, should I get careless, will go whipping around the bath like a furious, spitting serpent, spraying water everywhere. Go figure.

CLASSES CONTINUE, FIVE SESSIONS a day, focusing on oral expression, oral comprehension, grammar, and pronunciation, one day blurring into the next. I again shock my favorite teacher, Cécile, when instead of telling her I often fly (*voler*) I say I often steal (*voler*). Cécile has been working with me daily on my miserable vowel pronunciation, at one point drawing a clever but simple two-dimensional chart that indicates the shape of the mouth (from open to closed) along one axis and the origin of the sound (from the back of the mouth to the front) on the other. She writes the various vowel sounds in the appropriate places. The most difficult enunciations for me are the ones in the corners, the extremes.

"The French use the entire mouth when they speak," Cécile explains, pointing to each corner of the chart and having me watch her as she pronounces the sounds. "In English"—she draws a circle in the middle of the chart—"all of your vowels come from here." As validation, I can tell when I'm getting closer to the proper French enunciation of some vowels because my slightly chapped lips, which are not used to being stretched to such extremes, actually hurt when I hit the right note.

By Thursday, my lips sore from vowels and my throat raw from searching (in vain) for the letter *r*, the fog of French has descended heavily over my brain. Lost in the haze of thirteen-hour days, I'm desperate for the weekend to come, but for the next two days I'll have to work even harder, for my class of three is down to a class of two. The school, concerned about James's approaching entrance exam in Fontainebleau, has pulled him out of class for private tutoring.

I'm concerned about him, too. He may be a talented financial analyst, but he's learning French very slowly and speaking it even slower. When James speaks, he starts, like all of us beginners, before he knows how he's going to finish, as if the brain says, Let's just get going, kid, and we'll figure out the rest by the time we get there. But we don't, of course, and we all do idiosyncratic things when we hit the inevitable block. I clench my eyes shut for added concentration, which must look really weird; James pauses for what seems an eternity, his eyes wide behind horn-rimmed glasses, his mouth hanging open. He'll say, "*Il ahhhhhhhhhhhhhhhh*," as if he's showing his tonsils to a doctor while searching for the right vowel before finally switching in mid-uvula to "*ayyyyyyyyyyyyyyyyyyy.*" When we're outside, our speech accompanied (sometimes almost drowned out) by the nonstop buzzing of cicadas in the trees, I worry that one of them will fly into his open mouth. A few have bounced off me. Still, James seems as relaxed as ever, hanging out by the pool every afternoon, working on his tan instead of his conjugations.

THURSDAY NIGHT FEATURES A lecture about the French economy, only a few words of which I am able to grasp. After an hour of nuclear power, iron ore, and farming, we move to the dining room, where the conversation turns once again to *l'affaire DSK*. The hotel housekeeper who made the accusation has lost much of her credibility, and it looks as if Strauss-Kahn may be released, but the latest development is that a French journalist has just lodged an attempted-rape complaint against Strauss-Kahn. This has the effect of making her the most despised woman in France, while simultaneously sending DSK soaring even higher in the polls. Go figure.

Though I could hardly follow the economist's earlier lecture, now as he discusses *l'affaire* with us, I mysteriously find myself comprehending a good bit. The French are furious with the American judicial system for holding DSK "hostage." He's a prominent figure, not a flight risk, and shouldn't be treated this way. Emboldened after four days of classes, I decide to give a rebuttal in defense of my country. I rehearse it in my head several times, then speak up.

"I've a proposition. You give us Roman Polanski and we'll give you DSK." My French is decent enough that the room erupts in laughter.

SATURDAY MORNING THE SCHOOL nearly empties out. Karen, the New York retiree with whom I've become friendly, and I decide to take the bus into Villeneuve-lès-Avignon, a town that sits across the Rhône from the more famous and crowded Avignon, for a day of sightseeing. After a long wait, a bus arrives, but the driver waves us away. The bus is "full" (meaning there are no empty seats, but tons of standing room). The next bus isn't due for another two hours. Karen pleads with the driver to let us on and stand. Full? In New York, this bus would be considered half-empty.

"Another bus is coming in ten minutes," he promises, showing ten fingers to make sure we understand.

"You swear?" Karen asks, crossing her heart for emphasis. He swears. We wait for ten minutes, then twenty, then an hour, before we realize that the bus driver was speaking another universal language, one that, like the periodic table, knows no borders or accents: the language of deceit.

We reach Villeneuve-lès-Avignon by taxi, and Karen and I, having pledged to speak only French to each other (a promise only occasionally broken), spend a pleasant day visiting the deserted hilltop gardens of a monastery established in the tenth century and an ancient, peaceful cloister. Millefeuille is Karen's second immersion experience. Two years earlier she'd attended a school near Nice for a full month, and she's been taking classes in New York on and off since.

I've been curious why a seventy-something-year-old is working so hard to learn French. The story comes out in dribs and drabs. Her initial, somewhat unconvincing response is that she wants to visit her daughter, who is currently living in the French-speaking nation of Cameroon. But as we wander through the ancient grounds of abbeys and castles, among the long dead, I can't shake a weird feeling that we are not alone—that a third party is stalking Karen, staying mostly in the shadows but never losing sight of her, while at the same time propelling her forward.

The stalker is revealed over lunch.

"I'm two months short of being declared a cancer survivor," Karen tells me in English. She expresses outward confidence that it's not coming back, noting that all her tests have been encouraging, but her actions say something else. As we pass shops, she shows no interest in going in ("I've stopped buying things;

I'm getting rid of stuff at this point"), and later she talks about all she wants to do in the next couple of years, finally letting her guard down and admitting, "I don't know how much time I have." Karen has made her list, and learning French—for no other reason than to learn French, to conquer something that has eluded her for life, something beautiful and desirable—is at the top.

Karen is determined to learn French before she dies.

FRENCH-LANGUAGE BOOT CAMP ENTERS its second week, and the new arrivals—a pair of diplomatic attachés from Slovakia, another pair from Ireland, and three Germans—are a convivial group, but I miss James and the other students. I have to admit, though, that it's nice being a veteran, showing the new kids the ropes, even joking with the teachers as my French gradually improves. Bicycling during a lunch break on one of the bikes provided by the school, I see two women from class walking down the street. "*Bonjour, mesdames!*" I call, waving, as I pass, nearly swerving into a truck and ending my French quest prematurely.

After dinner, Cécile organizes an activity in the garden, and much to my delight, I'm able to cross one item off my list of French goals: playing *pétanque* in France. It's a fun match, I play well, and no one has to kiss Fanny.

As the week continues, I become increasingly aware that my brain's processing speed is, as linguist David Birdsong had predicted, slower than that of the younger students. But we all get tripped up, even on what should be the simplest things. Inger Stevens, it turns out, has spent *three semesters* studying French at the Sorbonne, yet I witness her having trouble with the simple sentence "I went there," specifically with the placement of the pronoun "there" (*y*). She insists it should be *Je suis y allé*, rather than *J'y suis allé*, which happens to be the same mistake I'd made two hours earlier. Translated literally either as "I there have gone" or, as Inger preferred, "I have there gone," the phrase sounds wrong either way to the American ear. God knows how you say it in Swedish (actually I asked, and it's not pretty: *Jag gick dit*), but in English both versions sound as if you're speaking mock Amish.

Inger and the instructors agree that French is difficult to learn, even for the French. On Inger's first day of French class at the famed university in Paris, she was handed a set of colored pencils, which are employed to help students (of all ages—the same method is used in French kindergartens) ensure that their nouns, verbs, and adjectives agree in gender, subject, and number.

I ask one of the instructors who speaks English (as well as Spanish) whether she thinks English or French is easier to learn. "Oh, English!" she says without hesitation. It's a much simpler language, she explains, without all the conjugations and rigidity of French. The grammar was a piece of cake. Her biggest problem in learning English was the strange pronunciation (I imagine she's referring in part to *r*'s that don't originate from your rectum) and the vocabulary. The English language, she says, has many more words to be learned than the French.

This seems like an opportune time to bring up with the instructor one particular word that I've observed the French don't have. *L'affaire DSK* has sparked a debate in France—and at Millefeuille—about how women are treated in society. French women may be famed for their seductive powers, but it's powerful men who seem to benefit the most from the seductions, taking mistresses and perpetuating one of the largest economic gender gaps (another term the French no have equivalent for) in Europe.

The word that I find conspicuous for its absence is "wife." The French have a word reserved for "husband" (*mari*) but not for "wife." The word for wife, *femme,* means both "woman" and "wife," depending on the context. So a man refers to his wife as "the woman" or "my woman." Maybe this is a stretch, I say to the teacher (with the assistance of some hand motions, because "stretch" is a word I don't know in French), but do you think there's a connection between the language and the culture? Put another way, does the absence of a dedicated word for "wife" reflect a French woman's status?

She says no, not at all; we do have a word, *épouse* for the wife and *époux* for the husband.

But that's not the same thing, I argue. Those are just the masculine and feminine forms of the generic word "spouse."

We have the word "spouse" in English, too, I say, but we also have distinct words for "husband" and "wife" that have no other usage, and you have only the one for "husband."

She gets it. I can see the change in her eyes, as if a curtain has just been lifted. After a moment of thought she adds that, come to think of it, the same is true for sons and daughters. A son is a *fils,* but a daughter is, once again, just a girl, a *fille.* Say *fille* and you could be talking about either your daughter or the girl who milks the cows. The instructor puts her pen down and sits back with an amazed look. "Never occurred to me," she says, her voice and eyes full of wonder, and I have a feeling she may well continue the conversation with someone else—perhaps her *mari*—down the road.

It is Thursday night, my last dinner at the school, but one I've been looking forward to, for tonight's lecture is on wine, and the speaker has brought along quite a few bottles of local wines for a *dégustation,* or wine tasting, to accompany his talk. It's sure to beat the lecture on the French economy. We taste four Côtes du Rhônes, learning how to appreciate them, examining the color, swirling the wine in the glass and again in our mouths, tasting with and without food, before and after aerating. All very serious stuff, yet in the middle of this I notice Karen desperately trying to suppress convulsive laughter, her body literally shuddering. She slides a bottle toward me, its label printed in both English and French. The English reads,

The vintage is resulting from the assembly from Viognier type of vines and white Clairette 88 years, entirely collected with the hand, in cases. That gives a wine of yellow color pale with flavours of fishings and fruits white. To be useful between 10 and 12°C, with aperitif, with foie gras, cooked fish or white meats.

By the time I hit "flavours of fishings," I'm in the same boat as Karen. For Francophones, here's the original French:

Cette cuvée est issue de l'assemblage de cépages Viognier et Clairette blanche de 88 ans, récoltée entièrement à la main, en caisses. Cela donne un vin de couleur jaune pâle avec des arômes de pêches et des fruits blancs. Servir entre 10 et 12°C, à l'apéritif, avec du foie gras, des poissons cuisinés ou des viandes blanches.

Ah, the delicious irony, to be in a language class, struggling to learn French, and to see how badly a commercial enterprise can screw up translating a wine label. It looks as if they either did a word-for-word translation or used an early version of a computerized translation program (the wine was bottled in 2008). You have to wonder why, with all the bilingual Frenchmen around, they didn't take ten minutes to run it by someone first.

Out of curiosity, I later bring the not-quite-empty bottle to my room and type the label into Google Translate to see how a contemporary machine translation compares to the vineyard's. Here's what it returns:

This cuvee is a blend of varietals Viognier and Clairette blanche 88, harvested entirely by hand, in boxes. This gives a pale yellow wine with aromas of peaches and white fruits. Serve between 10 and 12°C, aperitif, with foie gras, cooked fish or white meat.

Not bad. Other than lacking the words "as an" before "aperitif," the translation is pretty decent. Most importantly, it correctly translated *pêches*. The winery's mistranslation stems from the fact that *pêche* has two different, unrelated meanings: "fishing" and "peach."

With only a day of classes left, I've allowed myself to get quite drunk at the tasting and the dinner that follows. The standard two-week stay at Millefeuille feels like just about the right duration. One week is too short, and after two weeks you're ready to hang yourself from the nonexistent shower-curtain rod if you have to face one more day. The immersion approach is assumed by everyone in the field to be the best way to learn a language, and it probably is, but there's a fine line between immersion and drowning.

Since midway through the second week I'd been feeling the fatigue getting in the way of learning, making embarrassing high-school-freshman errors, saying *de le* instead of *du,* for example. I even contemplated cutting class one day and taking a train to the coast for a break, but my conscience (and the substantial per diem investment) kept me in my seat. Karen and I, the oldest two in the group, are struggling the most, but

I've seen it in the eyes of all the other students as well. Except for James, who, right till the end, was as calm, relaxed, and unperturbed as ever.

Inside the bubble of this isolated school, it's hard to tell how much French I've learned, speaking only to teachers and other students, but this weekend I'll get an idea, for, like James, I have my own exam of sorts: dinner in Paris with my French-rocker pen pal, Sylvie. After thirteen months of study, am I capable of holding a conversation with, not another student or a teacher, but a Frenchwoman? This is the acid test, a much-anticipated Paris meeting, and my very *raison d'être* all rolled into one. As I finish off the Côtes du Rhône, savoring its hint of trout, I check my e-mail, finding a deflating note from Sylvie.

> How are you? I'd like to tell you for the 16th, we can't
> come in Paris and I'm so Sad for this because my fiancé
> and I have a lot of things to pay and my car to repare.
> If we come in Paris, It will be very difficult to end the
> month. Please Bill, don't blame me, we'll see you the
> next time :).

Merde. Now I'm drunk *and* depressed. No dinner in Paris, no shopping. No *conversation*! Oh well, what are you going to do? I compose a reply, hiding my hurt, trying to sound casual. Before I can hit the "send" button, I feel a tap on my shoulder.

"Guy! What the hell are you doing here? I told you, we're through!"

"What the hell am *I* doing? What the hell are *you* doing,

chéri? Giving in as easy as that? I'm disappointed in you."

"You see her note. What would you like me to do?"

"For starters, you could go to Orléans."

"No way. This is obviously just a cover story. And if I offer to come down, negating her excuse of the expense, it puts her in an awkward position."

"And?"

"And what?"

"And what's the problem with negating her excuse? It's she who's breaking the date, not you. Go ahead, *put* her in an uncomfortable position. Make it *hard* for her to refuse, not *easy*! This is a exactly how you've been approaching French—afraid to take risks, afraid to fail! Take a train down, have a couple of drinks, see if you can actually speak French to a couple of real, live French people, and take the next train back to Paris. You've added an extra day to your trip for this meeting; you've come four thousand miles. You're going to just let it vanish?"

"I don't know . . ."

But deep inside I know that my swashbuckling alter ego is right. About everything, and some of it stings. I check the train schedule. Sure enough, Orléans is only an hour from Paris. I delete the reply I was writing and start over with my offer, signing the note "Guy."

Cherchez la Femme

. . . .

RICKY: Honey, you can't go running around Paris all by
yourself.

LUCY : Why not?

RICKY: What about your French?

LUCY: What about my French?!

RICKY: Well, Paris is a big city, and not knowing the
language, you're liable to get in a lot of trouble.

—*I Love Lucy*, 1956

Paris! Merely to look at the word evokes a visceral response
unmatched by virtually any city in the world. Prague, London,
Warsaw, Istanbul: beautiful as they may be, do any of them
elicit an emotion? Think—no, even better, *say*—the word
out loud: *Paris*! What do you see? What do you feel? For me,
the word conjures up the Eiffel Tower, bridges over the Seine,

outdoor cafés, the glistening gold dome of Napoleon's tomb. Stately monuments and ancient streets. Corner *boulangeries* from which the smells of freshly baked bread waft every time a customer opens the door.

Paris! The adopted home of Ernest Hemingway, Gertrude Stein, and countless other writers and artists who have been drawn here for centuries. Just wandering a few blocks from my hotel in Saint-Germain-des-Prés, I pass plaques commemorating the former residences of Albert Camus and George Sand, a sundial created by Salvador Dalí. This, I remind myself, is why I've been studying French. *This* is what it's all about.

Reclining in one of the comfortable public chairs in the Luxembourg Gardens, which are in full, magnificent bloom, I watch the comedic ballet of solo tourists from every corner of the globe trying to take photos of themselves: balance the camera, set the timer, race into position, view the disappointing result, and repeat. I've seen this before, of course, but for the first time it occurs to me why the photographer-models are so reluctant to simply ask another tourist to take a photo: the language barrier.

As for my own language barrier, the thrill of being in Paris brings out my inner Guy, and I address every waiter, hotel clerk, and shopkeeper I come across in French, even though in this touristy section of Paris virtually all of them speak far better English than I speak French. I'm quite the chatterbox, asking to try on a beret, inquiring about the price of a sweater.

Easy stuff, although I know I'm speaking atrociously, but what two weeks of immersion has given me, as much as anything else, is confidence, which is half the game, it turns out, and a self-perpetuating one.

As I dine al fresco under an awning, I even take a stab at putting together the request, "Can I change my table? The wind is blowing the rain onto me." It isn't easy, taking me several minutes to compose in my head before I'm ready to signal the waiter. The biggest stumbling block is, surprisingly, the first two words of the request—"can I"—because I've forgotten the conditional tense for *pouvoir,* an easy, common word that I knew well before I started class two weeks ago but that is now jumbled up with so much other material I can't locate it in my attic-brain. Totally blanking, I resort to running down the memorized list of conjugations for *pouvoir* in my head, in order, the way you do when someone asks you which letter comes before *s* in the alphabet.

I can't help noticing that no other tourist in the restaurant is making a similar effort. They just plop down and address the waiter in English, simply assuming that he should speak *their* native tongue in *his* country. Now, I don't expect everyone who wants to spend a week in a foreign country to follow my example and first spend a year studying its language, but, I want to cry out, would it kill you to at least say "hello" and "thank you" in French? Surely, you already know those words! My irritation finally hits a fever pitch on Sunday morning in the hotel restaurant. I am sitting alone with my coffee and croissant when a family comes in.

"Good morning," the woman says cheerily to me.

"*Bonjour,*" I reply, which provokes an embarrassed *bonjour* from her. Great, I've made my point. Still, I could make it better. I am about to gently chide her by pointing out, in French, "We are in France; we should speak French, no?" but I bite my tongue. Fortunately so, for a moment later I hear the family chatting among themselves—in French. They are a French family visiting Paris and, correctly assuming I was non-French, spoke English to me as a gracious courtesy. *Mon dieu,* am I becoming an insufferable language snob?

If so, payback is on the way, for that afternoon I am on a train headed to Orléans to meet, *to speak with,* Sylvie and her fiancé, Antoine. Yet before I so much as open my mouth, I need to handle a major dilemma that I've been dreading for days, one that makes the *vous/tu* uncertainty seem trifling by comparison. Do I greet Sylvie with a handshake or a kiss?

And when I say "kiss," I mean that cheek-to-cheek air kiss, where you touch cheeks and make a smacking sound with your lips as if you were actually kissing, which in most cases you are not, then repeat on the other cheek. And it doesn't always end there. The French, it seems, are so fond of the kiss that they sometimes go for three or even four, depending on the region. In general they kiss twice in the north, and anywhere from three to a tongue down your throat in the south. As with the formal and familiar terms of address, this is socially important, so important that the French have a protocol reminiscent of *tutoyer* to assist in resolving any doubt: you ask. That's right, you say something like, *On va se faire la bise?*

On the one hand, I guess it's nice to have a direct and un-ambiguous way out of the uncertainty, but under no circumstances are those going to be my first words to Sylvie at the train station! Knowing I had to deal with this, I'd asked Cécile for advice before leaving Millefeuille. She'd taken my conundrum very seriously and, in a process reminiscent of my *vous/tu* decision tree, had gone down a list of questions to divine the correct protocol: How long have we been corresponding? Are we *tutoyer*-ing? What valedictions do we use in signing our e-mails? When I was done, she had concluded, "Kiss." Certainly Guy wouldn't do anything but kiss, but frankly, I'm not sure which of us is holding the train ticket.

One thing we are not going to do, by the way, is hug. I've observed that the French don't hug socially. They just don't. This may be because they don't have a word for it. They used to—*embrasser*—but somewhere along the way the terms of endearment all got ratcheted up one level, and *embrasser* now means "to kiss," a real kiss, on the lips. *Baiser,* which used to mean "to kiss," is now the vulgarity "to fuck," although it can still mean "to kiss," depending on the context.

Well, there'll be none of that kind of talk at the Orléans train station, where I easily recognize Sylvie from her Facebook photos and take the plunge, confidently initiating a two-cheek *bise* before shaking hands with her fiancé, Antoine, saying, "*Enchanté.*" This is the last intelligent thing I will say in French for the rest of the day. As we walk out of the train station, Sylvie says something to me in French. "*Pardon?*" I ask, not catching it, so she says it in heavily accented English.

"*Non, non, en français,*" I say. "*Mais plus lentement.*"

She repeats, as I've requested, more slowly.

Huh?

She repeats again.

Whazzat?

Finally, returning to English, she says, "I was just trying say, 'Thank you for coming to Orléans.'"

Oh, of course. I knew that, I lie. But Sylvie and Antoine speak differently, rapidly and more colloquially than the Millefeuille instructors or the waiters, who are used to dealing with tourists, and I can hardly make out a word from either of them.

We make our way through the streets of Orléans, where in 1429 an illiterate teenage girl named Jeanne d'Arc drove out the occupying English army, an event still celebrated annually. Orléans, Antoine tries to explain to me in French, is famous for something else. I have no idea what until Sylvie presents me with a gift. As the Meetup class clown might've said, I may not speak French, but candy I know. Orléans, Antoine tells me, is the birthplace of pralines, the confection made of almonds and caramelized sugar, and the company that made these has been manufacturing them using the same recipe since the sixteenth century.

We make our way through town, Antoine, a graduate student in history, serving as proud ambassador and guide, leading us into shops and past statues and fountains, until we reach an outdoor café at the foot of Orléans's Gothic cathedral, which, three centuries older than the pralines, is in only slightly worse shape. Sylvie and Antoine do both seem genuinely glad to see me, convincing me that Sylvie's financial excuse for not coming to Paris was sincere. It is a beautiful afternoon in a beautiful city, exactly how I'd imagined this long-anticipated meeting to be—if, that is, you substitute Antoine for Sylvie, and English for French.

Neither French nor Sylvie have made much of an appearance as we sip some very strong Belgian beer (Antoine's civic pride does not extend to the local brew). I keep trying to switch to French, but Antoine would like to actually converse, so he keeps reverting to English, and after a while, exhausted, so do I. His impression of the United States has been formed largely from TV shows such as their favorites, *Supernatural* and *Smallville*, which sounds hazardous at best, and he has many questions: What movies and TV shows do Americans watch? Why so many jokes about New Jersey? (That's a hard one to answer—New Jersey is just . . . funny.) Why are you treating DSK like a criminal? Oh, jeez. Here we go again. "Our system of justice is different in France," he says. "Here, you are presumed innocent until proven guilty."

Now wait a cotton-pickin' second, I want to protest. We practically *invented* that phrase while your ancestors were lopping off heads in the Tuileries! But I let it drop, because the French newspapers have been indignantly reporting the headlines (FRENCH WHINE, FROG LEGS IT, PEPÉ LE PEW, BOOTY GAUL, and CHEZ PERV, to name a few) running in the New York tabloids, which have already tried and convicted Strauss-Kahn, and I figure the less I say about this whole business, the better.

Antoine goes on about the differences between French and American attitudes regarding sex and politics. "We had a president who died in the bed of a prostitute."

"We had a governor," I reply, "who died in the bed of his mistress."*

I take one more shot at switching the conversation back to English and Sylvie. The same woman who's been writing me long, warm, chatty e-mails for the past few months has barely said a word. It's like I'm with a different person. "*Et toi,*" I say, trying to draw her out, "*tu voterais pour DSK?*"

She thinks for a moment before giving a shrug and finally saying one of the few words she will utter all day. "Puh!" I'm not sure whether this means "Hard to say" or "I have no idea what you just said."

"*Mon français est très mauvais,*" I apologize.

"But you write so well in your e-mails."

---

* Nelson Rockefeller.

"I'm a writer," I joke (or half joke), rather than confess that I spent hours on each note. Exhausted from gabbing, Sylvie lets Antoine continue the conversation as we order another round of beers. Antoine and I chat some more about this and that, he in English, and I, as much as I can, in French, and Sylvie has been so quiet for so long that it occurs to me there might be a good reason.

"Do you understand Antoine when he speaks English?" I ask in English.

"Yes, I understand most."

"And when I speak French, do you understand me?"

"No."

QUEL DÉSASTRE! I TAKE the train back to Paris, numbed over my inability to converse in French. I hope that James fared better on his exam in Fontainebleau.* Why, I wonder, can I converse with a waiter but not with Sylvie and Antoine? And I realize that there are two kinds of French: there's *situational* French, the kind taught in all the courses, and then there's everything else. Situational French makes good use of all those little clusters you've learned (*est-ce que je peux, j'ai besoin de*) and you can substitute a word here or there to borrow a pen, try on a hat, or move your table. Yet the French of "everything else," the French of normal conversation, requires vocabulary, grammar, and, especially, speaking and oral comprehension

* In fact, I'm delighted to say that he passed.

skills that I've barely scratched the surface of in my hundreds of hours of study.

I shouldn't have been surprised at my difficulty speaking French with Sylvie and Antoine, for even after two weeks of immersion, while I could (usually) place pronouns in the proper position and figure out whether to use the *passé composé* or the *imparfait,* I still couldn't understand much from the school's guest lecturers or even the other students. Perhaps I expected too much from Millefeuille. Looking back, I'd say that whatever you come in doing, you leave doing a little better. Students who arrive speaking a little French leave after two weeks speaking a little more French. Those who come in speaking excellent French, like Inger Stevens, leave speaking even more excellent French. As for me, when I came to school, I didn't speak French. I still don't speak French, only now I don't speak it *better.*

Did I give immersion in France enough time? Would I have learned French if I'd stayed at Millefeuille another two weeks or two months? Based on the French of the two students there who'd previously done four weeks of immersion, I'd say, maybe if I'd stayed for another two years. *Deux ans.* Or is that *deux années?* And why do the French have two words for "year" but the same word for an office and the desk *in* the office?

How can anyone be expected to learn a language like that!

The next day, my last full day in France, my situational French does at least allow me to locate and buy a ticket to a concert at Sainte-Chapelle, the stunning Gothic church on the

Île de la Cité, a small island that sits in the Seine, and the site of the original settlement of Paris. With the setting sun streaming in through the soaring stained-glass windows, I listen to a quartet performing Vivaldi's *The Four Seasons,* the strings resonating magnificently throughout the chamber. I hear the silvery pizzicato notes depicting tinkling ice in the "Winter" concerto, the "drunkards falling asleep" in accordance with Vivaldi's instructions for "Autumn," and the languor of "Summer."

I recognize them all, and it seems fitting that my trip to France, to learn a language, ends here, where music written four hundred years ago by an Italian composer and performed by French musicians speaks clearly to this twenty-first-century American. I take some solace in discovering, in the most unexpected and beautiful of places, yet another universal language that, like deceit and the periodic table, spans centuries and cultures. And one that even I can comprehend.

TWELVE HOURS LATER, I am on the rail shuttle approaching Aéroport Orly for my flight home. As the train pulls into the South Terminal, a garbled announcement seems to be saying that this is the last stop, everybody off! But, *un moment, s'il vous plaît.* This isn't my stop; the train's supposed to continue to the West Terminal—my terminal. I exit with the other passengers into chaos—crowds, police, long lines. Something is going on. Must be yet another *grève* over the retirement age. Using a word I have down pretty well by now, I ask a young woman from my train car, who is wearing a backpack and a very disturbed expression, "*Quel est le problème?*"

She says something about *une bombe*.

"*Vous avez dit 'une bombe'?*" I repeat, disbelievingly. Even more disbelievingly, finding myself performing another famous Inspector Clouseau routine ("You said . . . a *boomb*?"). Well, not an actual bomb, most likely, but a bomb threat, enough to shut down the shuttle to the West Terminal but, mysteriously, not the terminal itself. The young woman looks at her watch; I look at mine. She asks an airport employee for assistance getting to the West Terminal as I tag along, accompanied by a third person from our train, an Asian student in the same predicament. The Frenchwoman gets an explanation in rapid French, then summarizes it in simpler French for us. There is a bus. However, because of the *boomb* threat it will take a long time to reach the other terminal, and, I figure based on recent experience, the bus is sure to be full, or at least the French version of full.

I have an idea. Forgetting for a moment that I can't speak French, like a man who temporarily acquires a strength he didn't know he possessed when he sees his wife pinned under a car, I suggest, "*Nous pourrions prendre un taxi,*" tossing off a conditional tense and gurgling four *r*'s!

"*Mais, c'est cher,*" she says.

"*Mais pas pour trois.*" There are three of us to share the cost. We step outside, and the Frenchwoman approaches a taxi.

After a brief conversation, she reports that the driver says he's not allowed to take fares between terminals. She glances at her watch and, looking like she's going to cry, starts back to the terminal.

"*Attendez un moment,*" I say to her. And then to the driver: "*Combien?*"

He shakes his head. "*Désolé, il n'est pas permis.*"

There's one more universal language we haven't touched on yet. "*Vingt euros,*" I offer, pulling out a twenty. I guess I *have* come a ways since having to pay for train tickets twice on my previous trip to Paris. "*Pour juste quatre minutes!*"

He looks around to make sure no one is watching.

"*Trente.*" Ten euros apiece to catch our flights. A bargain.

A few hours later, midway across the Atlantic, the bilingual stewardess addresses me in French, then apologizes and switches to English. "*Pas de problème,*" I say with some pride. "*Je parle un peu de français.*" Well, as much as I needed to catch this plane, anyway.

Eyes Wide Shut

. . . .

On ne voit bien qu'avec le cœur. (We see well only with the heart.)
—ANTOINE DE SAINT-EXUPÉRY, *Le petit prince,* 1943

"It's bizarre," Dr. Chinitz says of the arrhythmias I get only while lying down, a phenomenon I'd just reproduced in his exam room. "I've never seen anything like it." These are not comforting words, especially coming from a man who's done, by his count, ten thousand cardiac ablations. "Let's put you on a monitor for a few weeks and keep an eye on it."

I silently groan. I'd worn one before, and it's no fun, having wires attached to your chest 24/7 for weeks and being tethered to a customized cell phone that sends data to a monitoring center. The device arrives on Monday. On Tuesday I get a call from Dr. Chinitz's office. "The doctor would like you to come in tomorrow." There must be some mistake, I say. I haven't even worn the damn thing for a full day. No mistake. He wants to see me tomorrow.

I didn't think God, much less the Heart Rhythm Center, could get me an appointment with Chinitz in a day, but they add me on to the end of his schedule. "Come in around six." This is one hardworking man.

I DON'T STOP TO play *pétanque* this time. The waiting room is empty, the office strangely calm and relaxed, like the atmosphere after a thunderstorm, and I'm seen almost immediately.

Chinitz greets me warmly. "Have a seat."

He opens my folder. "I'm concerned about what we're seeing on your monitor," he says, showing me the EKG.

To my eye it looks like the same region of the Pyrenees that every other EKG I've ever seen looks like. "It's hard to be certain because the monitor has only four leads, so we don't get a complete picture, but some of these have the signature of ventricular tachycardia." Yet another piece of percussion added to my rhythm section. But the word "ventricular" replacing "atrial" sounds sharp even to my untrained ear.

"This could be very serious."

"How serious?"

"You could experience sudden cardiac arrest."

Sweet baby Jesus in velvet shorts!

"I know you've been through a lot, and I hate to put you

through yet a third procedure, but ventricular tachycardias are very different from atrial. We really need to go in and do another ablation, this one in your ventricle. And sooner rather than later."

I nod. "How soon?"

He looks at his watch. *That* soon?

"It's too late to get you on tomorrow's schedule. Can you come in Friday?" he says, using the same casual tone as my auto mechanic scheduling a tune-up.

Thirty-six hours from now. "I suppose I could clear my schedule."

The rest of the appointment, the rest of the day, is a blur. I'm pretty sure this did *not* happen, but in my reconstruction I'll always remember Chinitz standing up at that point, firmly grasping my hand, and with a twinkle in his eye, saying in French, "*Courage!*"

FRIDAY TAKES FOREVER TO arrive. But to make sure it does, I resolve not to lie down before then, not for ten seconds, so as not to trigger any arrhythmias. I sleep, or try to sleep, sitting in a chair both nights, but every little extra or missed beat from my heart stirs me awake, and I find myself thinking of television's Fred Sanford looking to heaven, hand to heart, crying, "Oh, this is the big one! You hear that, Elizabeth? I'm comin' to join you, honey!"

When that grows old, I dwell on the sobering fact that I've

been walking around with a lethal condition for months, and I visualize the headline in my town paper: LOCAL WRITER—no, make that HUSBAND OF LOCAL PHYSICIAN DIES OF BROKEN HEART IN FRANCE. GRIEVING WIDOW: "IT'S WHAT HE WOULD'VE WANTED."

Is it really? Suppose I don't make it to Friday—I almost certainly will, or Chinitz would've found a way to get me into surgery sooner. But suppose I don't. Is a single-minded devotion to learning French how I would've wanted to spend the last year of my life? Two o'clock in the morning, while awaiting a lifesaving heart procedure, is a good time to start being honest with yourself, to *parler à cœur ouvert.* The truth is, not only have I failed to become fluent, or even conversant, in French, but I've failed spectacularly—more so than I ever imagined possible. You can't say I haven't tried. Over thirteen months, I've completed all five levels of Rosetta Stone, Fluenz French, a hundred podcasts of Coffee Break French, two Pimsleur audio courses, a fifty-two-episode season of the 1987 PBS series *French in Action,* a weekend immersion class, social networking, a Sartre play in French, and a dual-language book, topped off by two weeks at one of the top language schools in France.

Sitting in the dark, wrapped in a blanket as the digital clock seemingly clicks forward one minute every three minutes, I wonder, Where do I go from here? Even if I want to continue pursuing French—and I'm not at all sure that I do—I don't know how much more time and money I'm willing to devote to this Sisyphean task. I figure that I've spent 900 hours—nearly double the 480 hours that the Foreign Service Institute estimates is required to achieve basic conversational ability—studying French. And that's not counting the hundreds of hours spent watching French movies and television and listening to French radio, not casually, but actively, trying to decipher what I was hearing.

What else could I have done with those hours? Well, in just the first forty I could've built that garden shed I've needed for years. Then I could've finally gotten around to reading Proust. Tutored a struggling local student. *I could have learned golf!* There is a golf course right across the street from me. That's what older guys do, not French. Why didn't I use the time to learn golf instead?

As proof that God has a sense of humor (as well as a peerless sense of timing), I'd returned from France to find the current issue of the *New Yorker* opened to an essay by Larry David, of *Seinfeld* and *Curb Your Enthusiasm* fame. Reflecting on his failure to achieve even mediocrity in golf despite half a lifetime of trying, he writes that he has finally come to accept that "I was never going to be good. Never. Think what I could've done with all that time. Learned French."

This Is Your Brain.
This Is Your Brain on French.

All second languages are learned out of love.
—JULIA CHO, *The Language Archive*, 2009

I open my eyes, which is a mistake, because what I see looks and feels like the inside of a coffin. The panic attack swelling inside me, making the space even smaller, is quelled by a soothing male voice: "*Et le petit prince eut un très joli éclat de rire qui m'irrita beaucoup.*" A week after Dr. Chinitz, in a seven-hour procedure, has exorcised the demon plaguing my heart, I'm back at work—not at my desk, but in the institute's imaging lab, squeezed into the narrow tube of the fMRI machine. I exhale, close my eyes, and listen to the clip of *Le petit prince* over the rat-a-tat-tat of the magnets.

Thirteen months ago, remember, before beginning my study of French, I'd had fMRI scans of my brain taken while listening to short texts in English, French, and Japanese—my native language, the one I was going to learn, and the one that was totally foreign to me—with the intent of repeating these scans after I'd learned French. Fresh out of Millefeuille, I figure my French may never be better than it is now, so I'm back inside the fMRI machine to complete the experiment.

I'm particularly interested in the two areas of the brain most associated with language. The Broca's area is largely responsible for the production of language, although it also plays a role in comprehension (especially decoding syntax); the region known as the Wernicke's area handles language input, both spoken and written. Although we're using state-of-the-art equipment to examine these areas, their role has been recognized for over a century: autopsies of patients with aphasia, unable to express their thoughts in speech, often show damage to one or the other of these regions.

After I've completed the scans, a colleague processes and analyzes the images on his computer, coming up with some interesting results, particularly in the French/Japanese comparisons. Here's a look at my brain a year ago, before I started studying French. It's a composite image of the left side of my brain created by comparing the neural activity while listening to French to the neural activity while listening to Japanese. The dark areas indicate where there is comparatively greater activity during the French audio clip. As you can see, there's only a smattering of it; that is, a year ago my brain was processing French pretty much the way it was processing Japanese.

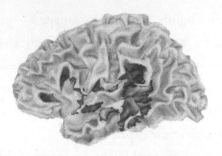

French vs. Japanese: Before

Here's what the same composite image looks like now, a year later. Notice how much more of the brain is "lit up" while listening to French. After a year of studying, "my brain on French" no longer looks anything like "my brain on Japanese." *Formidable!*

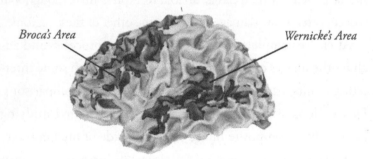

Broca's Area   *Wernicke's Area*

French vs. Japanese: After

The increased activity is especially high in the Wernicke's and Broca's language centers, and while we can't see it in this image, the right side of my brain—where the reasoning functions of language, such as intonation and emphasis, are handled—

shows much more activity as well. Clearly, *something* positive happened, and while I didn't totally comprehend the excerpt from *Le petit prince,* I did pick up more phrases this time, and the reading just seemed less foreign, more familiar, and that's probably what the brain activity is reflecting.

No linguist or neuroscientist would seriously suggest using an fMRI scan as a measure of language acquisition, but last year I'd also taken a baseline college language-placement exam. My score on that written, online test, which measured comprehension and grammar, was 310, not quite qualifying me for first-year college French. I retake the test and am surprised to see that I've scored 418, just two points shy of admitting me to third-year French. Thus in a year of study I have, by this measure, learned the equivalent of two college years of French. So I am making decent progress if we ignore the oral and aural parts.

Sans doute I do know quite a bit more French now. The size of my vocabulary has increased by an order of magnitude, and given enough time (a critical qualifier), I can conjugate all the regular and many of the irregular verbs in the most common tenses. And I *did* navigate an airport bomb threat and a dentist.

But here's the thing: While I have learned a lot *of* French, I have not learned French. And that is a major distinction. I have always subscribed to the maxim, have always taught my children, that with enough effort, anything can be accomplished, at any age. As an adult I've acquired the skills of woodworking and baking. But language, as has been suggested, does seem different. I wonder whether it is in fact a child's game, limited by a critical period. Was I simply too old to learn French?

Not necessarily, according to linguist David Birdsong, who, after listening to my progress report, tells me, "It's not too old for anything in the sense that it is, I think, a disservice to the species to not put yourself out there and try to do your best at whatever it is that you're doing. Yes, the odds are getting stacked up against us; it doesn't mean we can't push back." Nevertheless, he says, "Your level of motivation, and effort, and dedication to this, should've paid off more. But there are a lot of individual differences that come into play, which is not at all the case in first-language acquisition."

That is, *everyone* learns their first language, but when it comes to second languages, there is huge variation. And I want to be crystal clear about this: *My failure to learn French should not deter anyone else from trying.* For to do so is not only a "disservice to the species" but a disservice to yourself, and you may have a great deal more success than I had. You may even become fluent. Some people have a gift for languages and some don't.

Elissa Newport, who first proposed the second-language critical period theory, is less surprised at my lack of proficiency. Some years ago she'd followed the English progress of Chinese college students who'd immigrated to the United States. "They have these times of quantal jumps," she says, "but you don't see anything approaching fluency until about five years out." And these are *young* men and women. What about a fifty-eight-year-old?

Was there ever any hope for me? "Sure," she says. "If you had lots and lots of immersion . . . for five to seven years, you'd get to be pretty damn good." *Five to seven years of immersion?* There's another term for that: *moving to France.* Let's see, if I can convince Anne to give up her medical practice and retire to France when we're sixty-five, I'll be fluent by the age of just . . . seventy-two. Keep dreaming.

My Millefeuille classmate Karen is in her seventies and still, to her great credit, pursuing *and learning* French. If I blame my failure on age, how to explain her success? I'd figured that in two weeks of classes, given the advantage of my relative "youth" and my intense preparation, I'd catch up to her, but I never did. My theory is that, while both of us had taken French in high school and let it disappear from our lives for decades, I had dropped it after only the tenth grade, while Karen continued throughout high school and a year of college. Those extra few years she gained on me decades ago, while we were both within the second-language critical period, made, I think, a huge difference. My theory, then, is that the age at which you're trying to master the language as an adult is less important than how much time you spent with it in childhood and adolescence, no matter how long ago that might have been.

I mention this to Birdsong, who confirms that studies suggest that age and duration of first exposure are critical, and you retain more of the language than you realize. Even forty years later, the language is still there in your brain, a sleeping giant, waiting to be awakened. Unfortunately, my giant kept hitting the snooze alarm, and I may be kidding myself that enduring a couple of more years of Madame D—— might have made a difference.

Perhaps this project was doomed from the start. All those hours down the drain, and between the shocks, the anesthesia, and the French, I probably got dumber to boot. A year ago I'd taken a cognitive-function exam, and my low scores had me concerned about more than learning French. I'd been below average in nearly all of the ten categories, with alarmingly low scores on two critical tests, landing in the bottom 10th percentile on the composite memory test and in the lowest 5 percent for my age group on the visual memory test. How much lower, I wonder, as I gloomily prepare to retake the exam, can I go?

"ANNE! ANNE!" I FLY down the staircase, two and three steps at a time.

She hears the commotion and comes running to meet me, braced for whatever emergency she's about to face. "What happened?"

I'm catching my breath.

"Is everything all right?"

I wave a piece of paper. "Everything's fantastic! You're not going to believe this!"

My cognitive scores have skyrocketed. I am now above average in seven of the ten categories, and average in the other three. My word recall, or verbal memory, score has shot from the bottom half to the 88th—*the 88th*—percentile! But hold on: some of that effect is surely due to employment of those memory techniques I'd learned, including constructing a memory palace for the words that were being flashed at me. Yet I had no such technique for the visual memory test, where one has to memorize abstract shapes—boxes inside triangles, that sort of thing. And on that test I've leaped from the bottom 5th percentile to the 50th.

As for the most important measure, my total score, here's what a year of French has done to my brain: my neurocognition index has gone from the 55th percentile, just about average, to the 84th, a significant jump.

Studying French has been like drinking from a mental fountain of youth!

COGNITIVE SCORES

		BEFORE FRENCH	AFTER FRENCH
——	Word recall	40	88
- - -	Visual memory	5	50
— —	Neurocognition Index	55	84

We fellow baby boomers have been seeking this elusive fountain of youth with more determination than Ponce de León, as we try to avoid becoming the Alzheimer's generation, spending billions of dollars on brain exercise games and adult piano lessons.

I revitalized my brain merely by studying French. And as a bonus, I can order dinner in Paris. A disappointing year? This may have been the most significant year of the rest of my life, as I've stumbled quite by accident across the strategy to keeping my brain sharp and functioning as I move from middle to old age. What had felt like Waterloo has instead become a rousing victory, with implications so startling, so important, I can almost overlook my failure to learn French.

FRENCH: BEAUTIFUL, MADDENING, TENACIOUS. It won't let me win, but it won't let me go. I have no potatoes in my Hudson Valley kitchen, only the more poetic *pommes de terre*—apples from the earth. Instead of a slice of lime—*bah, ouais!*—I top off Anne's *côté voiture* with *citron vert*—smiling to myself that the French call it simply a "green lemon." I text Katie often in easy French—*ça va?*—and she responds likewise, a game we can't stop playing, as if we share a secret code.

I may not have learned all the French I wanted to, but what I did learn has enriched my life immeasurably. Yet perhaps the most important French lesson learned over the past year is this:

you can love a thing without possessing it. Even as French has eluded me, my ardor for the language has only grown. I love, and will always love, French. Whether it loves me back, I have no control over.

Je ne regrette rien.

Lagniappe

· ·

A Louisiana French word unknown in France, a lagniappe
is a little extra measure thrown in by a merchant (such as a free
thirteenth doughnut when a customer buys a dozen).

Last night I dreamt I was French. As before, this mainly involved sipping absinthe at the window of a dark, chilly café,
wrapped in a long scarf that reached the floor, legs crossed,
Camus in one hand and a hand-rolled cigarette in the other.

But this dream continues, as Anne slips into the booth, giving me a *bise* on each cheek, while *la serveuse* places a café au lait
in front of Anne before she even has her coat off.

"*Madame le Docteur,*" *la serveuse* says, smiling.

"*Merci, Catherine.*"

"*Avec plaisiirre,*" she says with a wink.

Anne, of course, has no medical license in France but, not ready to retire, has found another, unofficial calling in the picturesque but remote Provençal village that we've made our home.

"*Tout va bien?*" Catherine asks, and everyone in the café leans in to hear the answer.

Mother and daughter are fine, Anne replies in perfect French, which my smartphone translates into English for me. Although the phone says it was touch-and-go for the veal. I guess it meant the calf.

"Did Dr. Chinitz help out?" I ask.

"No, dear. He's not in this dream. You don't need him anymore."

Anne has been to the *marché*. I peer inside the bag, which is overflowing with bright orange carrots, crimson tomatoes, beets the color of a sunset, baguettes, a freshly killed duck, and a half kilo of foie gras, the last item a gift from the grateful farmer.

"I ran into Jean-Claude," Madame le Docteur says between sips of her café au lait. "He asked if you want to go rabbit hunting on Sunday."

Baah, ouais! My mouth starts watering like Elmer Fudd's.

A rap on the window. It's Minnesota le Gros, my *pétanque* partner, with an armload of *boules,* motioning with his chin for me to come out and play.

"Uh-oh," Anne says, hustling out. "I'd better warn Fanny."

On the sidewalk I see Sylvie and Antoine, pushing a stroller with their twins, Guy and Alexandre. "*Bonjour,*" they call. I smile and wave. In the background, Mont Ventoux looms majestically, its pinnacle tantalizingly hidden behind a wispy white mist, a cloud of milk in a cup of tea.

I glance at my watch. Like Anne, I need to keep busy in retirement, and I've also found a calling. My two-hour lunch over, I walk to the schoolhouse, passing a *pâtisserie.* My New School instructor, Marc, in apron and toque, runs to the door, crying, "*Ploo de gâteau!*"

At the school a packed classroom of adults, seemingly half the town, awaits my arrival.

"*Vous avez un stylo?*" a student asks.

"Madame D——," I scold her, "no French, please. This is an English class." She pulls herself out of class by the ear.

"But English is so difficult!" another student cries. "Your *r*'s are impossible, you have too many words, and we are too old for this." A murmur of assent, then in unison the class says, "We are never going to learn this language!"

The mob starts to advance threateningly.

"*Écoutez!*" I say. "*C'est vrai, nous sommes âgés. Mais nous pouvons repousser.*" We can push back, I tell them, my accent so atrocious that the mob starts giggling, some collapsing to the floor. Seizing the moment, I jump onto the desk, thrust a fist into the air, and give one final battle cry to my language students.

"*Courage!*"

SOURCES

· · · · · · · · · · · · · · · · ·

Begley, Sharon. *Train Your Mind, Change Your Brain.* New York: Ballantine Books, 2007.

Bellos, David. *Is That a Fish in Your Ear?: Translation and the Meaning of Everything.* New York: Faber and Faber, 2011.

Birdsong, David. "Age and the End State of Second Language Acquisition." In *The New Handbook of Second Language Acquisition,* edited by William T. Richie and Tej Bhati, 401–24. Bingley, UK: Emerald, 2009.

———. "Second Language Acquisition and Ultimate Attainment." In *The Handbook of Applied Linguistics,* edited by Alan Davies and Catherine Elder, 82–105. Carlton, Australia: Blackwell, 2004.

Brown, Roger, and Albert F. Gilman. "The Pronouns of Power and Solidarity." In *Style in Language*, edited by Thomas A. Sebeok.

Cambridge, MA: MIT Press, 1960.

Bryson, Bill. *The Mother Tongue: English and How It Got That Way.* New York: William Morrow, 1990.

Buzan, Tony, and Barry Buzan. *The Mind Map Book: How to Use Radiant Thinking to Maximize Your Brain's Untapped Potential.* New York: Dutton, 1994.

Child, Julia, and Simone Beck. *Mastering the Art of French Cooking: Volume Two.* New York: Knopf, 1970.

Deutscher, Guy. *Through the Looking Glass: Why the World Looks Different in Other Languages.* New York: Holt, 2010.

Foer, Joshua. *Moonwalking with Einstein: The Art and Science of Remembering Everything.* New York: Penguin, 2011.

Fuller, Graham E. *How to Learn a Foreign Language.* Washington, DC: Storm King Press, 1987.

Golinkoff, Roberta M., and Kathy Hirsh-Pasek. *How Babies Talk: The Magic and Mystery of Language in the First Three Years of Life.* New York: Dutton, 1999.

Gruneberg, Michael M. *French by Association.* Lincolnwood, IL: Passport Books, 1994.

Higbee, Kenneth L. *Your Memory: How It Works and How to Improve It.* New York: Marlowe, 1996.

Horne, Alistair. *La Belle France: A Short History.* New York: Knopf, 2005.

Johnson, Jacqueline, and Elissa Newport. "Critical Period Effects in Second Language Learning: The Influence of Maturational State on the Acquisition of English as a Second Language." *Cognitive Psychology* 21, no. 1 (January 1989): 60–99.

Krupa, Grazyna. *Expulsion: The Story of Acadia.* Toronto: Canadian

Broadcasting Company, 2004.

Lodge, Anthony R. *French: From Dialect to Standard*. London: Routledge, 1993.

Lorayne, Harry, and Jerry Lucas. *The Memory Book*. New York: Stein and Day, 1974.

McCullough, David. *The Greater Journey: Americans in Paris*. New York: Simon and Schuster, 2011.

McWhorter, John. *Our Magnificent Bastard Tongue: The Untold History of English*. New York: Gotham, 2009.

Nadeau, Jean-Benoît, and Julie Barlow. *The Story of French*. New York: St. Martin's, 2006.

Pei, Mario. *How to Learn Languages and What Languages to Learn*. New York: Harper and Row, 1966.

Pinker, Steven. *The Language Instinct: How the Mind Creates Language*. New York: William Morrow, 1994.

Pressley, Michael, and Joel R. Levin. "The Keyword Method of Recall of Vocabulary Words from Definitions." *Journal of Experimental Psychology: Human Learning and Memory* 7, no. 1 (Jan 1981): 72–76.

Roubaud, E. *The French Language: A Complete Compendium of Its History and Etymology*. London: Crosby Lockwood, 1879.

Rymer, Russ. *Genie: An Abused Child's Flight from Silence*. New York: HarperCollins, 1993.

Sera, M. D., C. Elieff, J. Forbes, M. C. Burch, W. Rodríguez, and D. P. Dubois. "When Language Affects Cognition and When It Does Not: An Analysis of Grammatical Gender and Classification." *Journal of Experimental Psychology: General* 131, no. 3 (September 2002): 377–97.

Shattuck, Roger. *The Forbidden Experiment: The Story of the Wild*

Boy of Aveyron. New York: Farrar Straus Giroux, 1980.

Spence, Jonathan D. *The Memory Palace of Matteo Ricci*. New York: Viking, 1984.

Strauch, Barbara. *The Secret Life of the Grown-Up Brain*. New York: Viking, 2010.

Sturges, Hale, II, Linda Cregg Nielsen, and Henry L. Herbst. *Une fois pour toutes: Une révision des structures essentielles de la langue française*. 2e éd. White Plains, NY: Longman, 1992.

Timoney, Charles. *Pardon My French: Unleash Your Inner Gaul*. New York: Gotham, 2009.

Wade, Nicholas, ed. *The Science Times Book of Language and Linguistics*. New York: Lyons Press, 2000.

ACKNOWLEDGMENTS

. . . .

French, which, as we know, couldn't muster up a dedicated word for "wife," has more ways to say "thank you" than President Mitterrand had mistresses. For example:

Je voudrais exprimer toute ma gratitude to the many individuals who greatly enlightened and enlivened my linguistic journey, including linguists Heidi Byrnes and David Birdsong and psycholinguist Elissa Newport, all of whom graciously lent their time and expertise to lengthy interviews and follow-up questions; Bowen Zhou of IBM and Jeff Chin of Google for their patient demonstrations and explanations of machine language translation; Acadian historians Lise Pelletier, Anne Chamberland, Don Lévesque, and James Lavertu; polyglot Benny Lewis for his insights on adult language acquisition; Rosetta Stone's director of learning, Duane Sider; Connie Klein, for sharing her own experiences with learning French; and Karen Nolan for her advice on cognitive testing.

Un grand merci à mes collègues Dave Guilfoyle, Matt Hoptman, Jan Hrabe, and Raj Sangoi for permitting, conducting, and interpreting fMRI results on my pre- and post-French brains.

For my retelling of the history of French *je suis redevable* to the work of Jean-Benoît Nadeau and Julie Barlow, whose excellent book *The Story of French* provided much of the source material.

Mes remerciements à Amy Gash, mon éditrice formidable, qui ne parle pas français mais qui maîtrise bien l'anglais!; publisher Elisabeth Scharlatt and the entire creative and marketing team at Algonquin Books for their support and contributions over three books; *agent et amie* Liz Darhansoff; and *copain* Jack Fuchs for his valuable insights and manuscript suggestions.

Bien sûr, je tiens à remercier ma femme, Anne, and ma fille, Katie, for once again allowing their personages to grace these pages despite their (mostly) unvoiced reservations, and for putting up with a hopelessly French-wannabe husband and father.

Finalement, to Dr. Larry Chinitz and the entire staff at NYU Langone Medical Center, *je vous remercie de tout cœur.* I thank you with all my heart.

À bientôt!

AVAILABLE NOW

'Life itself is the proper binge' **Julia Child**

When Julia Child arrived in Paris in 1948, a 'six-foot-two-inch, thirty-six-year-old, rather loud and unserious Californian', she spoke barely a few words of French, and didn't know the first thing about cooking. 'What's a shallot?' she asked her husband Paul, as they waited for their sole meunière during their very first lunch in France, which she was to describe later as 'the most exciting meal of my life.'

As she fell in love with French culture, buying food at local markets, sampling the local bistros and taking classes at the Cordon Bleu, her life began to change forever, and we follow her extraordinary transformation from kitchen ingénue to internationally renowned (and internationally loved) expert in French cuisine. Bursting with Child's adventurous and humorous spirit, *My Life in France* captures post-war Paris with wonderful vividness and charm.

About Julia Child

Julia Child was born in California and worked for American intelligence during World War II. Afterwards she lived in Paris, studied at the Cordon Bleu and taught cooking with Simone Beck and Louisette Bertholle, with whom she wrote the first volume of the best selling classic *Mastering the Art of French Cooking* (1961). She died in 2004.

SEE THE MAJOR MOTION PICTURE
Julie & Julia
WRITTEN FOR THE SCREEN AND DIRECTED BY NORA EPHRON
STARRING MERYL STREEP AND AMY ADAMS

My Life in France

Julia Child
with Alex Prud'homme

'Exuberant, affectionate and boundlessly charming'
The New York Times

'Lively, infectious... Her elegant but unfussy prose pulls the reader
into her stories'
Chicago Sun-Times

'Captivating... Her marvelously distinctive voice is present on every page'
San Francisco Chronicle

AVAILABLE NOW

Multilingualism is on the rise – in the coming decades, as many as two billion people will learn English as a second language. The next stage up from multilingualism is the domain of the 'hyperpolyglot' or 'superlearner': someone who claims to know at least six languages. But what does it mean to 'know' a language? Can a person claim to speak a language fluently if it isn't their mother tongue? What role does culture play in learning languages?

In this accessible and enthralling book, Michael Erard discusses the upper limits of the brain's capacity to learn languages and sheds light on the 'hyperpolyglot' phenomenon, from the Italian cardinal Giuseppe Mezzofanti, who was said to speak as many as seventy-two languages, to the 'superlearners' of the 21st century. Erard's exploration spans the globe as he travels to meet these living marvels and to investigate those of antiquity, and his discoveries not only illuminate the intellectual potential within all of us, but also indicate how we might begin to unlock it.

About Michael Erard

Michael Erard has an MA in Linguistics and a PhD in English from the University of Texas, and has taught all around the world. His essays and reviews have appeared in *The New York Times*, *Science*, *Wired* and *New Scientist*. He is the author of *Um...: Slips, Stumbles, and Verbal Blunders, and What They Mean*.

'You'll be awed by the incredible characters in this eye-opening book.
How do they do it? And what can the rest of us learn from them?'
Joshua Foer, author of Moonwalking with Einstein

'Part travelogue, part science lesson, part intellectual investigation,
[Mezzofanti's Gift] is an entertaining, informative survey of some of the
most fascinating polyglots of our time'
The New York Times

'Michael Erard has written the first serious book about the people who
master vast numbers of languages – or claim to ... he approaches his
topic with both wonder and a healthy dash of scepticism.'
The Economist